Guru j

Guru Jesus

Robert Van de Weyer

LONDON
SPCK

First published 1975
by S.P.C.K.
Holy Trinity Church
Marylebone Road
London NW1 4DU

Printed by offset in Great Britain by
Hollen Street Press Ltd, Slough

SBN 281 02873 7

*To the
People of Christ Church
Lancaster*

CONTENTS

INTRODUCTION

This book is a diary of the process which led me from the agnosticism of my upbringing to becoming a disciple of Jesus Christ. It is based on essays, diaries, and letters written over the past eight or nine years which I have now drawn together and amplified. As the title indicates, I became a follower of Jesus by regarding him as a Guru. I recognised him as a supremely wise and happy man, and, in the Hindu tradition, gave him my complete and unquestioning obedience so that he could show me the way to wisdom and happiness. It was only after making Jesus my Guru, and after clumsily trying to follow his instructions on prayer, that I gradually came to believe in a supernatural God.

This climax, however, is not reached until the last part of the diary during my second visit to India. The first two parts record the gradual process of development which brought me to the point where I was able to submit my life to Jesus. When the diary opens I was in the first year of the sixth form at a public school in central London. I was a weekly boarder, going home each weekend to my parents in Hampstead.

PART 1
Schoolboy

Last Sunday night I couldn't get to sleep. Lying awake I began to look at the months and years ahead, at the prospect mapped out for me, hoping, I suppose, to find some underlying purpose. I found the opposite.

For the next two years my eyes will be fixed on A-levels: plodding through textbooks making notes, writing essays to learn by heart, doing countless practice questions as the exams draw closer, and finally, for three sweaty hours, pushing my pen furiously across an examination script. Then, if the anonymous examiner sees fit, I'll spend a further three years at university, absorbing more facts and learning more essays by heart. And if my degree is good enough, I'll leap straight onto the second or third rung of the career ladder, as an accountant, a civil servant, or even a school teacher. For forty years I will work hard, relieved only by three weeks' annual holiday lying in the Mediterranean sun. My salary will gradually increase, my belly spread, and my vision narrow, until at sixty-five I receive my reward: a few sleepy years of retirement, cutting the hedge and pruning the roses, until death.

The prospect doesn't appeal to me. So why should I bother with A-levels? Why should I follow the cream of society into university and up the career ladder? I have been brought up to believe in the virtue of doing good to others, and yet the course of life planned for me is entirely selfish. At this point in my thoughts I finally dropped off to sleep.

On Monday after school I went for a long walk through Hyde Park to try to think it through more clearly. It was cold and I was wearing only a jacket, but the act of walking, the steady brisk rhythm, made me oblivious of the temperature and of everything around me. For about an hour and a half I was totally absorbed in my own thoughts, an experience I've never had before. What is the purpose of life? At first, after imagining various people — my parents, the teachers, my friends — each asking me that question, I answered: to be happy oneself, and to make other people happy. But then I imagined Mr Ralston, my economics teacher, a young man with dark, curly hair and trendy clothes, peering through his black-rimmed spectacles, saying: 'What obligation is there for you to do good to others? Give me a single reason why you should ever inconvenience yourself to help someone else.' Perhaps it is a trick question, but I couldn't think of an answer. Of course I can think of circumstances in which you do someone a favour so that he'll do a favour in return, but that can hardly be called unselfish — it's division of labour, as Mr Ralston would say.

So, if I have no obligation towards others, then the sole purpose of my life is to make myself happy. In which case, why don't I leave school and set about enjoying myself? Now I imagined my father, sitting at the head of the dinner table with a glass of wine in his hand, remonstrating: 'But what if everybody thought like you? If everybody was pursuing his own selfish ends, the world would collapse into anarchy, and no one would be happy.' Possibly so, but so long as everyone doesn't think like me, then I can pursue my own happiness with impunity.

Now I did start to notice the cold, and I found my toes were stinging and my body shivering. By the time I arrived back at school I could think only about a hot bath and supper.

For the past four weeks my mind has been going round in endless circles. My thoughts seem to bash against the side of my head, and I have a recurring headache above my temples. I rarely fall asleep in less than an hour; I time myself by the strikes of Big Ben, and half-past-eleven or quarter-to-twelve are usually the last ones I hear.

You would think that the question 'What is the purpose of life?' would be the most important thing on the school syllabus. In fact it's never mentioned. Yet masters, like everyone else, are quite happy to make strict judgements about what is right and wrong. How can you talk about right and wrong without first thinking out the overall purpose of life? An action can surely only be called right if it helps you towards that purpose.

About eighteen months ago I was suspended from school for half a term for shoplifting. For the previous six months I had been going to Soho and Oxford Street and stealing anything that took my fancy — records, clothes, art books, sheet music, recording tapes. All in all I must have taken about a hundred pounds' worth of goods. Most of the things I didn't particularly want and I gave them away to friends, but I enjoyed the adventure, and of course it made me popular among the other boys at school. Eventually a teacher heard about it, my friends were interrogated, and the whole story came out. Luckily the headmaster decided not to expel me, and he telephoned all the various shops asking them not to prosecute. But what sticks in my mind now are the grillings I received, first from my housemaster, then the headmaster, and finally my parents. All were visibly horrified at my actions. My mother was in floods of tears, my father was rigid with shock, and even the ex-R.A.F. housemaster was hoarse and shaking with

5

emotion. And they each asked the same questions, almost in the same words: 'Surely you understand the difference between right and wrong? Doesn't your conscience tell you that stealing is wicked? Don't you feel guilty at what you have done?'

The same thing happened a term later when I was caught cheating in the summer exams. Tears came to the headmaster's eyes as he told me to take down my trousers for a beating. My housemaster afterwards said gruffly, 'I hope at last you feel thoroughly ashamed of yourself', and announced that in his opinion I should have been expelled from such a respectable school.

Fortunately I wasn't clear-headed enough to say so at the time, but the answer to all their questions is quite simple. I don't know the difference between right and wrong. I didn't feel any guilt at stealing and cheating. The word 'conscience' means nothing to me, and the only shame I felt was in the humiliation of being caught and punished. The reason why I don't continue to steal and cheat is that, as I looked in the mirror at the blue rings on my bottom, I realised that life would be easier if I stuck to the rules.

Are guilt and shame the only things which hold society together and prevent it from sliding into anarchy? Do people refrain from murder, rape, arson, theft just because doing these things would make them feel awkward and uncomfortable inside? Am I the ugly duckling, the moral deformity who should be cast out from society because he has no conscience?

Perhaps the moral code of my 'elders and betters' is an elaborate middle-class hypocrisy. 'Doing good to others', or at least not obviously harming them, and insisting that others behave likewise, is a way of preserving status and privilege. Thus when a member of the privileged class like myself breaks the code and acts in an overtly selfish way, it threatens to expose the whole hypocrisy.

Certainly when I was suspended for shoplifting the school's great fear was that the story should reach the newspapers, and those boys who were thought to be sufficiently unscrupulous as to phone up the daily papers were threatened with severe punishment if they did so!

But this explanation doesn't fit my parents. Though they are rich they condemn the inequalities of society, and throughout their adult lives have worked for the Labour Party. They enjoy their wealth and privilege: we live in a large, luxurious house with a tennis court in the garden, the food is lavish, wine flows every evening, and my two brothers and I have been sent to an expensive school. Yet they sincerely want to destroy the system which allows them to behave like this. They are not hypocrites because they admit the contradiction between their beliefs and practice and confess (admittedly without much breast-beating) their own weakness in not voluntarily giving up their privilege. But why are they concerned with the plight of poor people? Why do they go out at every election, summer or winter, to persuade others to vote for the destruction of the goose that lays such golden eggs? Why does my mother go each day to the slums of Paddington to help the West Indian immigrants? Last Sunday night at dinner I asked them these questions. They were embarrassed and a little annoyed, and lamely replied, 'Because we feel it to be morally right.'

My parents are atheists and seem to regard religion as an insidious Tory device to maintain the status quo. The religious answer to my questions, as I understand it, is that you should do good to others because this will please some mysterious, invisible entity called God, and God will eventually send you to heaven as a reward. This at least is honest, since doing good in order to go to heaven is openly selfish. But why should humans imagine that such a God exists? The proofs for the existence of God strike me as just word play. To say, for example, that the existence of the universe implies a creator, and that the creator is God, is equivalent to saying that the existence of the chair I'm sitting on implies a carpenter, and since I know nothing about him I shall call him Smith! Even if you prove his existence it wouldn't follow that God took pleasure in seeing human beings acting unselfishly towards each other. Judging from the way he has planned history, it seems more likely that he enjoys seeing men fight and kill one another.

The only remotely acceptable answer I have heard is from Mr Ralston. He too is an atheist, criticises the 'bourgeois values of the Establishment', and believes in a classless society. A few weeks ago he took a group of us for coffee at his home. He lives in a dingy bed-sitter, with moth-eaten old furniture and flowery wallpaper peeling off the walls, above a boys' club in the East End, and he spends most of his spare time organising ping-pong, dances, and basketball for the local toughs. He says that unless we, the middle classes, strive to bring about social justice and equal distribution of wealth, then we should expect to be destroyed when the working classes in this country, and the starving millions in Africa and Asia, seize our wealth by force. In other words it is in our own best interests to help the needy. Mr Ralston himself is from a working-class background in Birmingham.

Personally I don't like Mr Ralston — I find him cold and superior — though I respect his arguments and the firmness of his convictions. But he has one vital thing in common with everyone else I know who believes, for whatever convoluted and dishonest reasons, in the principle of 'doing good to others': he is visibly not happy. He smokes incessantly, he rarely smiles, and his hands shake with frustrated nervous energy. In this respect he is no different from his sanctimonious fellow masters whom he openly criticises; nor from the poker-faced and embittered old clerics who come to preach the joy of heaven to us from the pulpit; nor from my parents, drinking wine with their right hand, while their left struggles to pull the glass away. If my elders and betters are unable to find contentment and happiness for themselves, then their moral principles are not worth the conscience they're written on.

My thoughts are becoming increasingly intense and un-clear. Even when for a short time my brain relaxes, something that someone says sets it whirring again. The other day in the car, for instance, my elder brother, who was driving, happened to say, 'I reckon it would be an advantage if we took this turning to avoid the traffic lights.' Immediately I started thinking: 'What exactly does "advantage" mean? What standards does one use to say one thing has an advantage over another?' Not that I was interested in the answer to that question; and yet I couldn't stop myself. And of course any question like that eventually leads back to the difference between right and wrong, and the purpose of life, which are the things which really obsess me.

If the ultimate purpose of life is to be happy, I should look at my own experience to see what gives me the greatest pleasure. And if I can find some general links between different pleasures, I can perhaps see how to make myself more happy.

There seem to be two types of pleasure. First the sensual pleasures — eating, drinking, sex, etc. — which last only so long as your mouth is full or the girl is in your arms, and in excess quickly rebound back in the form of a stomach ache, a hangover, or the late-night blues. Second the intangible, 'spiritual' pleasures — friend-ship, beauty, reading poetry, listening to good music — which, though usually less intense, last longer and leave no nasty aftertaste. One hardly needs to be a Greek philosopher with a long white beard to know that the root of happiness must lie in the second type. Yet what precisely is the difference between the two? What makes the spiritual superior to the sensual?

At last my thoughts are becoming clearer. My headache has lifted, and for the first time in weeks I feel quite calm.

The afternoon following the last entry, the school film society showed 'Cléo 5 à 7'. It is a love story, gracefully and simply told. When I came out I went for a walk through St James's Park, which was cold and deserted, with the sound of traffic a gentle hum in the distance. The icy air seemed to cut into my brain, slicing away all the ideas and half-baked notions that had been buzzing incessantly round my head. Then the thought came to me — the greatest pleasure in life is love. In other words, the most intelligent way of pursuing my own happiness is not to pursue it at all, but to pursue other people's happiness. Suddenly I realised that this was the answer to all my questioning. I literally jumped for joy, and shouted into the darkness at the top of my voice: 'HAPPINESS IS LOVE.'

Since then I have been struggling with the word 'love'. It is used in so many contexts with different shades of meaning, yet intuitively I know what I mean by it. I am aware that my own experience of love is limited: my friendships at school are based mainly on common interests — sport, the theatre, and so on — without any deep concern for each other's happiness. But I can see love clearly and powerfully in poetry and literature. *Howard's End*, for instance, portrays a group of people who are convinced that love could transform their lives, and are prepared to sacrifice everything to establish truly loving relationships. There is a beautiful short story by Tolstoy about an embittered old shoemaker who, on the inspiration of a few passages from the Bible, decides to invite into his hovel passing tramps who need food and warmth. For the first time in his

11

life, by entertaining these hobos, he feels joy in his heart, and this joy persists throughout the day, lightening the dull monotony of his work.

Of course the moral principles I have been brought up with are supposed to be based on love. By helping one another, and by refraining from doing harm, life is more pleasant for everybody. But good behaviour is not love, as I understand it, but the natural result of love. Love itself is the pleasure which motivates good behaviour. It is the joy that comes to people from caring for one another, and from knowing that they are cared for. Yet the extraordinary quality of love is that it spills over and enhances every other pleasure in life. This was the experience of Tolstoy's shoemaker, whose hovel became a palace in his eyes when shared with a needy tramp, and it is the entire theme of E.M. Forster's novels: 'Only connect . . . and both will be exalted.' Even in my own experience at those rare times when I have had a close friend, the activities we did together became doubly enjoyable.

The mistake of conventional morals is that they ignore the pleasure of love and emphasise good behaviour. Good behaviour, however, can equally be based on shame and guilt — the fear of doing wrong — as well as on love — the pleasure of doing right. From the parents' and teachers' point of view it is easier to encourage guilt feelings in the impressionable child, since fear is a child's strongest emotion. The result is that while society may run smoothly and its members refrain from murder, rape, and stealing, they will not be happy. Even the socialism of my parents or Mr Ralston harps on guilt and fear — guilt at being privileged and fear of class warfare — and the utopian socialist society would at best only be a more efficient version of the present capitalist one.

So I have formed my own alternative moral code:

1. To love as many people as you can, as much as you can.
2. To concentrate on the pleasure of love, and let good behaviour follow of its own accord.

This term I have been put in a bed-study with Andrew Kingsley. We have not been particular friends in the past. He is older than I am, and when I first came to the school he used to bully and tease me mercilessly. But now we are growing much closer.

Among our contemporaries at school Andrew has always been a star. He's good-looking, with broad shoulders, thick fawn hair, and flashing brown eyes. He has always had enough pocket money to buy the trendiest clothes and latest records, and he generally gets the prettiest girls at parties. And he's good at sport. His father is an actor, and Andrew has inherited the actor's temperament: he is liable to flare up at the slightest hint of an insult. But despite all this he is sensitive and perceptive, and enjoys good poetry and literature.

After about a week of term I let him read this diary (he's the only person I have shown it to), and afterwards we talked until one o'clock in the morning about the purpose of life and the meaning of love. First of all he couldn't accept that one's sole object in life is to make oneself happy, but equally he could see no reason why it isn't. Then he argued that if you take pleasure in doing good to others, it cannot be called 'doing good'. But eventually he agreed that this is precisely what is wrong with conventional morals: it is because they make such heavy weather of helping others, and make it so joyless, that they only spread gloom. When we resumed the discussion the following evening he suggested that if my idea of pleasurable love (as he christened it) means anything, we should be able to translate it into our own relationship and discover it for ourselves.

Since then we have been conducting an experiment. Each of us has tried to be as concerned with the other's welfare as with his own. So far it seems to be working.

On small practical things, such as who should clean out the room this week or who should have the desk nearest the window, whereas previously we would have squabbled, now we manage to agree. And in our discussions, say about politics or school matters, we are able to disagree without bitterness or ill feeling. In English, the only A-level subject we do together, we help each other to think out the plays and novels we are studying, and neither of us minds if the other gets higher marks for an essay. I realise there is a danger, cooped up in a boarding school, of homosexual feelings developing between us, but I think we have the strength to prevent this from happening.

We have begun to discuss the possibility of one day forming a community based on the principle of pleasurable love. I have read Bertrand Russell's summary of Rousseau's ideas, and it seems that Rousseau's ideal community is very close to what we want. To learn the art of pleasurable love men must first break away from 'civilised' society and its economic system which makes such love impossible. For example, in civilised society men are forced to compete against one another to earn a living, as capitalist economics says that ruthless competition maximises production. But how can a man learn to love his fellow if he is fighting against him for his bread? In communist countries competition is replaced by state control where one group of people gives orders to the rest. But, as Rousseau says, goodness and love cannot develop unless there is equality where all men make decisions together. Moreover both capitalist and communist societies judge their success by the volume of material goods produced. As a result they are constantly having to create new wants and desires, in order to consume the ever-growing array of cars, fridges, washing machines, packaged foods and so on which are being manufactured. Thus civilised society depends on destroying man's natural contentment and putting greed and cruelty in its place.

A society based on pleasurable love would have to be small enough for everybody to know each other by name, so that all economic exchange and co-operation could be conducted on the basis of personal relationships. This is because pleasurable love can only develop through personal contact. Since trading with the outside world would constitute an impersonal economic relationship, based only on common material interests, the community would have to be mainly self-sufficient, producing its own food, building materials, energy and so on. Decisions affecting the whole community could be made by true Athenian democracy, with everybody meeting together to discuss and vote.

The paintings of Gauguin, which Andrew has introduced me to, contain this vision of the ideal society. Gauguin found in Tahiti a community (since destroyed by the white man's avarice) which was truly loving. The soft, warm colours and the still, silent figures of his pictures express the calmness and contentment of the people. Of course they had the advantage of a perfect climate and abundant fruit falling from the trees. Yet surely the happiness they achieved is possible for every human being, whether he lives on a wind-swept Northumbrian coast or a South-Sea island.

I see that it's almost six months since I last wrote in this diary. I have just read my last entry, and it sends shivers down my spine. How could I have been so naive? Did I seriously imagine that we could ever form a community of love? I don't even know what the word 'love' means.

It must have been within a fortnight of the last entry that my relationship with Andrew began to turn sour, and by the end of term we were hardly speaking. They say it's the little things which count. The first was that he refused to share the coffee, biscuits, chocolates, and other goodies which his parents gave him each weekend to bring to school. In retaliation I would disappear on Saturday mornings when we were supposed to clean out our room. He grew jealous that I was usually given better marks for English essays, and I became jealous (as if I ever really cared!) when he was awarded colours for swimming. Soon everything one of us did — his smoking in bed, my taking my shoes off in the evenings — annoyed the other, and we seemed to be constantly glaring at each other in repressed irritation.

I now realise that a further cause of tension on my part was sexual jealousy. Every Monday Andrew would describe in detail his exploits of the previous Saturday night. Though I doubted whether much of what he said was true, I was too inexperienced myself to call him a liar. But what made it much worse was that I was attracted to Andrew myself. I am not a homosexual, but almost every public-schoolboy, locked up away from girls, has homosexual urges, and it so happened that mine were directed towards Andrew. I think he saw this, and it made him exaggerate his heterosexual adventures even more. My humiliation was grotesquely re-enacted a few weeks ago during a school production of *The Tempest*, when I played Ferdinand. Miranda, Ferdinand's

17

beloved, was played by a ravishing, would-be deb from the nearby girls' school. Andrew was Caliban, naked except for a ragged loincloth. At the curtain call Miranda and I had to hold hands and stare lovingly into each other's eyes, but as the curtain fell Andrew slipped round and took her back to his own dressing room.

Since last March I have had more 'experience' with girls, and I daresay I could stand up to Andrew better now. But the more experience I have, the more disgusted I am with myself. I dislike the usual small talk, and I try to have serious conversations with the girls I go out with. Yet my high-flown views on life and love are shown up as babbling hypocrisy as I contrive to end every date with a 'see-how-far-you-can-get' session on a park bench or in a deserted alley.

This term I have become 'roving reporter' for the monthly school magazine. I have had two interviews so far. The first was with a disenchanted peer, living in one corner of his gilded mansion, the rest of which he now opens to the public at great profit, with a park and a small fun-fair in the grounds.

When his secretary showed me into his vast study, with an oak banqueting table in the centre covered with accounts and letters, His Lordship was reclining on a tatty leather sofa at the far end, gazing at the ceiling. He is not the high-powered tycoon I imagined, but a bored, mildly discontented man, irritated by his own success. As a boy he was not allowed to mix with other children and was educated entirely at home — 'That's why I'm so nutty.' His father then sent him to live in London on an income of ninety-eight pounds a year to teach him the value of money. 'Instead it taught me the value of cadging.' When he inherited the mansion it was in chaos, with 'tables piled on chairs, and Rembrandts heaped on Canalettos'. But there were large estate duties to pay off plus £120,000 per year maintenance costs, so about ten years ago he began to turn it into a profit-making concern.

He clearly now coins money from his Rembrandts, animals, and hot-dog stalls, but he despises the visitors, particularly the American tourists who pay sixty pounds per head to dine with a 'real live lord'. He resents the invasion of his privacy, and yet he admits he loves the publicity and would not shut up shop even if he could afford to. I asked why he thought peers, himself included, had such a high rate of divorce. He smiled wanly and replied: 'I suppose it's because we have a rarity value and tend to do rather well with women.'

My second interview was with Joe, the attendant at

the gentlemen's lavatory beneath Leicester Square. He compares favourably with His Lordship: he has the same air of blasé disinterest, though with a Cockney accent, but pities rather than despises his visitors. 'I like people; that's why I've taken this job.' He allows the homosexuals, who stand at the urinals staring furtively at other men's penises, five minutes before he taps them on the shoulder. The balding men who emerge from the X films and lock themselves in the toilets he gives fifteen minutes before banging on the door. He helps the addicts who come for a fix back up the steps again. While I was with him a shiny-haired, spotty young man came in for a wash and brush-up. Joe handed him a half-crown and asked him to buy a packet of fags. 'That chap's a nut', he said as the man skipped up the steps. 'He thinks he's Elvis Presley, but he dosses down under the arches. But I trust him with me half-dollar, 'cause that's the way to treat people like that — trust 'em.' The man didn't come back, and as I was leaving Joe said, 'I've lost my half dollar. When he next comes in he'll deny everything. Still, you can't blame him.'

The lord and the lavatory attendant: alpha and omega, the rich man and Lazarus!

I still believe in the ideal of pleasurable love. Or at least I can't see a flaw in the argument for it. But I am no nearer to discovering it.

I have joined the Community Service group in the school, and for the past six weeks I have been visiting an old woman called Mrs Chambers in a basement flat near Vauxhall Bridge. This is about the only loving thing I do at the moment, yet there is no pleasure in it. She's aged eighty and lives in horrifying squalor. She has a single room nine feet square, whose walls are damp and peeling, and the floor is bare flagstones. The sheets on her bed are unwashed and her clothes stained with grease. Often when I arrive she is eating her meals-on-wheels, but she suffers from Parkinson's disease, and her hand is so unsteady that much of the food slops down her chin. She is small and hunched, with a wispy moustache and frizzy, uncombed hair.

Though her initial suspicion has now worn off, she never appears pleased to see me, and during our conversation she looks sourly at the table and answers mostly in monosyllables. But when I get up to leave she presses me to stay. She has a son living in Horsham who occasionally comes to see her, and whom she refers to as a 'good-for-nothing layabout'. Her neighbours, who pop in to see her every day, she calls 'drunkards and prostitutes'. Presumably she has had a bitter life, but contrary to what the Community Service literature tells you about old people wanting to talk about their past, I have yet to discover anything of Mrs Chambers' former life. I haven't missed a single week with her so far, and I suppose I am doing some good. But I am reaching the point where, as I knock on her door, I long for the neighbour to poke his head over the bannister and tell me she's died.

Last Sunday I interviewed a 'high Tory' Member of Parliament for the school magazine. He is a devout Christian who has entered politics 'to serve the community', including, one imagines, Mrs Chambers and her like. He lives in a beautiful Queen Anne house in London, surrounded by priceless objects: a china cabinet in the bathroom; in the hallway a budgie called Victoria perched in an exact replica of the Crystal Palace; and draped above his bed a silk canopy with a coronet on top. In the early hours of the morning when I saw him he had returned from an elegant ball at Strawberry Hill, and he described to me the duchesses and bejewelled ladies he had danced with. He believes in liberty and freedom of opportunity, and he says his ambition is to become Home Secretary in order to reform the penal code.

What does serving the community mean? If I have money and Mrs Chambers has none, then service surely requires that I share my money with her. I described Mrs Chambers to him, and he replied, 'Yes, society must find a way of caring for people like her.' But society is a mass of people, and, in any meaningful sense of the word, cannot 'care' for an individual.

Diane, my latest girlfriend, is barely five feet tall, has a round, appealing face, and has recently appeared in a children's television serial playing a ten-year-old gipsy girl. But beneath her child like exterior she seethes with earnest emotion, and on Sunday she took me on a Vietnam demonstration.

It was horrible. We congregated outside the Festival Hall, waiting for more than an hour while people arrived. Drab denims and sloppy jackets were the uniform for men and women alike, and all had grim, determined expressions. Diane changed visibly: her face hardened, her lips pursed, and her speech became subdued and monotonous as she talked about 'American fascist pigs'. Then the banners unfurled and the march started, along the south embankment and across Westminster Bridge. Soon the chanting began: 'Ho, Ho, Ho Chi Minh'. The veins in Diane's neck bulged as she strained her soft voice. I tried, but I couldn't bring myself to join in. At first I mouthed the words, and then I stopped altogether. When Diane saw this she turned, her eyes flashing with anger, and cried: 'Shout, shout, you soppy little baby.' As the march swung into Whitehall I allowed myself to become detached from Diane, and I slipped off across Parliament Square to St James's Park station, and took the tube back home.

Now I don't dare ring her up. I hadn't wanted to go on the demonstration in the first place because I can't share the militant spirit of political agitation. But I went in order to please her. Inside myself I am as passionately concerned about world politics as any of them. I do care about the slaughter in Vietnam, about starvation in Africa and Asia, about urban deprivation in the West. Even the devaluation of the pound and Britain's perennial economic crises worry me. I canvass for the Labour

Party at every election. The existence of people like Mrs Chambers pains me, and I object to the complacent sympathy of pious Tories. I remember my father taking me to a C.N.D. rally in Trafalgar Square with the waif-like figure of Bertrand Russell standing against the huge lions declaiming on the iniquities of war. At the end he asked everybody to take a pound from his wallet to offer it to the cause, and I was deeply impressed to see rise above me a forest of arms waving pound notes.

Political involvement is a form of love, directed towards masses of people of whom you can have no personal knowledge. And like any other expression of love, it demands self-sacrifice. It is painful to hear of the sufferings of others, however far away they live, and it requires time and energy to agitate on their behalf. But somehow political involvement should not be grim-faced and overloaded with hate for your opponents: it too must be made pleasurable. At a Vietnam demonstration there should be love, not hate, for the American 'pigs'.

I have started smoking pot. When I was visiting the Redfern Gallery in Cork Street to interview Patrick Procter, the artist exhibiting there, I met a leisured young aristocrat called James Lander, who was in the process of lavishing his surplus cash on the artist's latest works. He took me back to his house in Chelsea for supper, and afterwards a group of friends came round for a 'smoke'. Since then I have been back four or five times.

The first smoke simply clouded my head and made me ravenous for sweet things. To everyone's amusement I gobbled two cream buns in quick succession, despite having had a large supper. But now that I'm growing used to it I find it increasingly effective. It puts a new perspective on things, and when I'm high I feel capable of loving the whole world. I picture particular people in my mind — Mrs Chambers, Andrew Kingsley, a girlfriend — and try to analyse my feeling towards them. Though I remain aware of their nasty characteristics they seem to matter less, and their good qualities are highlighted. I have even found myself wanting to kiss Mrs Chambers warmly on the cheek! I recall situations and re-enact them in my head, and I am able to see how I could have acted so much better and more lovingly. But, of course, when the high wears off nothing has really changed.

On the last occasion I smoked I had been studying *The Ancient Mariner* that morning, and as I reflected on it, it appeared as a frightening allegory of human life. The mariner represents an ordinary individual, and the ship's crew his friends and colleagues. They have no control over the movements of the ship, whether towards the roaring icebergs of the south pole or the dry heat of the tropics. The mariner himself involuntarily shoots the albatross, the omen of good fortune, and is forced to carry the guilt of his own folly as the crew hang the dead bird round his neck. In other words, we are all at the mercy of chance and of our own inner drives, yet each of us must bear the consequences of his own actions. As the ship is becalmed the crew die one by one and the mariner is left alone, haunted by their staring dead eyes as they lie on the deck. Though he wants to die also he cannot. This symbolises the process of ageing: friends die off or are lost, the comfort of companionship disappears, and one is left with lifeless memories. The only happiness the mariner experiences is in sleep, for in his dreams the ship sails perfectly without need of wind. But the dream cannot last, and when he finally arrives back home he becomes imprisoned by the grim memories of his voyage, compelled to retell the story to anyone who will listen. This is the fate of old people, who at the slightest prompting joylessly repeat the tired anecdotes of their past.

A-levels are my current albatross. We are encouraged to believe they are good omens, heralding the joys of life at Oxford, Cambridge, or some lesser university. But in reality they are dead weights round our necks, blocking out thought and imagination. And the joys of university life, even if they are real, last only for three fleeting years before we are becalmed for the rest of our active lives in a career.

This morning a visiting bishop from South Africa gave an Easter sermon to the school in the school chapel. He was a small, round man with a high voice, and perched on the huge pulpit in the nave his bald scalp and beady eyes could just peep over the reading stand. Once the giggling had died down I began to listen to what he was saying. He was describing the story of Jesus Christ being arrested, tried, flogged, and executed, as if he were a Roman soldier looking on.

The utter calmness and peacefulness of Jesus had never struck me before. Throughout the last days of his life he never once lost his cool. He gave all the right answers at his trial; he didn't flare up in anger or show any bitterness when his clothes were ripped from his back and the crown of thorns placed mockingly on his head. Even when he was nailed onto the cross he could still feel love for those who were killing him. I can never be a Christian because I could never believe in a supernatural God, yet by the end of that sermon I was saying to myself: 'If only I could be a disciple and be content to follow what Jesus commands, rather than having to puzzle everything out for myself.' And then as we all trooped out through the cloisters I was seized with a rush of emotion. I thought of Margaret Schlegal in *Howard's End* saying: 'If I ever fall in love, I shall want to shout it from the roof-tops.' If I could ever become a Christian, I found myself thinking, I would run up the aisle and dance at the altar for joy.

This afternoon I went for a walk in the park to try to think more about the sermon. In fact I couldn't think rationally about it at all, but instead a rather curious daydream, like a silent filmstrip, started going through my mind. It began with a scene from the Gospels: Jesus with his apostles walking through the ripe yellow cornfields, plucking the ears of corn. Nearby there were some farm labourers harvesting the grain with sickles and a woman drawing water from a well under a tree. The sky was blue and there was a gentle breeze. Then gradually the sky darkened and the air became stagnant, the labourers and the woman faded away, the tree withered and blackened, and the land became a desert of grey earth. All the apostles fled in terror, and Jesus was left on his own carrying a large wooden cross. He walked slowly onwards, faltering slightly under the weight, and up a low mound of earth, placing his cross upright at the top. He then climbed onto the cross, stretched out his arms and died. I wasn't weeping, nor was I even looking at Jesus, but I was staring out beyond the mound, across miles of dark, barren desert. In the far distance I could just make out a range of beautiful purple mountains. And then the vision ended, and I found myself looking at the ducks in the pond!

I have no idea what the daydream means. I doubt if it signifies anything, except that at this moment the personality of Jesus holds a certain fascination for me. Considering the countless number of arid divinity lessons I have sat through, given by a chain-smoking cleric who is quite capable of comparing the joy of love with the pleasure of eating a tin of baked beans or hitting a half-century — to be still fascinated with anything connected with religion is in itself a miracle. Besides, since I can never become a Christian, I cannot have the luxury of following blindly the orders of another person.

I have spurned the advice of my masters and am not staying at school the extra term to take Oxbridge entrance. I cannot believe that all intellectual excellence is concentrated in two medieval cities, and I am prepared to take a chance on a vulgar red-brick seat of learning.

On the day term ended Andrew and I set off on a camping holiday in Ireland. Not having shared a study for over a year we had become the best of friends, but I'm afraid our friendship has barely survived three weeks together in a leaky tent surrounded by greasy pans and smelly socks. Almost every common decision sparked off an argument: who should drive (we both like driving); who should wash up (neither of us likes washing up); how far we should loosen the guy ropes when it rained; which route we should take. And our combined efforts to erect the tent on wind-swept sand dunes and peat bogs, with the pegs jumping out as fast as we could hammer them in, and the spring frame suddenly folding up around us, reduced us almost to blows.

We visited Powerscourt, a vast Georgian mansion near Dublin, where my grandmother was brought up. Unfortunately Granny married beneath herself, and now lives in comparative poverty in a detached house in Dorchester, with only a housekeeper to look after her. But, as she says, 'born an aristocrat, always an aristocrat', and she describes how as the eldest daughter her father used to send her out in mid-winter to take soup to his starving tenants. Despite his benevolence, however, he was a heavy drinker and gambler, as were his successors, and the estate was gradually sold off to pay debts, until a few years ago the present viscount sold the house and moved to England. Andrew and I had to pay five shillings to get in.

Most of the holiday we spent in the west, in Kerry and

Mayo, and our usual routine was that Andrew sat reading or sketching the scenery while I went off on long, lonely walks. During these walks I tried to induce what pot-smokers call the 'natural high'. The monotonous rhythm of my own plodding would absorb the natural fidgetiness of my body, and the quiet beauty of the green and purple hills, populated only by shaggy sheep and goats, would overwhelm my thoughts and emotions, so that I could feel completely peaceful and inwardly relaxed. In such a state all my worries — what my A-level grades will be, how to spend the next year before going to university, my feud with Andrew — appeared absurd and petty, and, as under pot, I felt I loved the world, however evil it might be. But, of course, when I returned to the tent we would soon be bickering again.

Since coming back I've been to James Lander's house a couple of times. He is off pot at the moment in order to write a book on 'pragmatic philosophy'. Pragmatism, apparently, judges whether something is true according to the usefulness of believing it is true. My clever answer to that, which didn't amuse James, was to ask whether it was useful to him to believe in pragmatism, the only consequence of which is that he feels compelled to write about it. In other respects, however, I am discovering that he has a ruthlessly pragmatic approach to life. Contrary to what I imagined, he inherited very little money and finances his smart house and luxurious life style by playing the stock exchange and dealing in slum property.

We discussed the significance of pot-smoking. James regards it purely as an escape, an amusement, but I feel it's more than this. The sense of harmony with the world which you can derive from pot is an imitation of the harmony and happiness which the man who is truly loving experiences; it is a foretaste of the ultimate goal of life. The same applies to the 'natural high', whether induced by beautiful scenery, or by music, or poetry. These imitations of real happiness can serve as boosters, strengthening your will to learn how to love. But the danger which the hippies fall into is to make the imitation into a substitute, treating pot-smoking as a kind of religion, an end in itself.

I spent the period until Christmas doing various jobs, partly for interest and partly to save money, while my university applications were being processed. My first job was on a battery chicken farm near Royston in Hertfordshire.

11 October '68

I am doing this horrible job as a result of grovelling to the Cambridge dons. I went to Cambridge for an interview in the hope of getting a place on my A-levels alone, without taking the entrance exam. They refused me, and on my way back I stopped off at Royston Labour Exchange. Now I am cleaning out filthy chicken pens for four shillings an hour, six days a week, under the orders of a bristly retired Colonel who has yet to speak to me in less than a hoarse bellow. And I have to pay a pound a week for the privilege of living in a battered old caravan surrounded on all sides by monster stinging nettles. It's no good my shouting 'Workers of the world unite'. No self-respecting worker would take a job like this in the first place!

When work finishes at five I have the rest of the evening to sit beneath my gas light and think about the meaning of happiness, interrupted only by a fry-up supper I cook for myself on the single gas ring. Philosophy is a great escape, and I find I can immerse myself in thought for over an hour at a stretch before having to stop to read a book or listen to the radio. Actually I haven't been thinking directly about happiness, but about the things which prevent happiness. As I try to establish loving relationships with people and observe the relationships of others, I become increasingly aware of all the human urges and desires which conflict with the desire to love, and which so often are stronger than it. These urges and desires are what Christians call sin, but the word 'hate' is more explicit, since they are the opposite of love.

Frequently hate is simply laziness or lack of courage, an unwillingness to accept the sacrifices which loving relationships demand. Or it may take the form of direct antagonism towards another person, as when you are angry, for example. But most often hate is hidden or disguised, and it requires considerable imagination to see it for what it is.

Personal ambition, for instance, the eighth deadly sin of the technocratic age, is acclaimed as a virtue among the middle classes. At school you are taught to try to do better than the others, to be top of the class or captain of the cricket eleven. Then in adult life striving to 'better one's position in life' and 'reach the top of the tree' is regarded as a sign of strength and manliness. Yet one man can only improve his position by forcing other men downwards, and the rivalry and competition on which our society thrives depend on the suffering of the weak. Jealousy, often the result of failed ambition, is a form of hate which is adept at clothing itself with justice. The man who envies the possessions or position of another convinces himself that he has a right to the thing he envies. The wife nagging at her husband for new carpets and furniture to keep up with the Joneses will find herself saying: 'But why should Mrs Jones have bright new furnishings while I have to make do with this shabby junk? It's unfair.' Jealousy destroys my relationship with Andrew, yet in every row each of us is convinced he has justice on his side.

The sincere effort to love can itself cause hate. The Vietnam demonstrators, in their desire to stop the killing of innocent people, generate hate for the American aggressors in order to further their cause. The possessive mother, trying to protect her darling boy from evil influence, bitterly resents the scruffy friends he chooses and the naive, radical views he adopts as he clumsily asserts his independence. The 'do-gooder' who selects the most needy cases on which to lavish her love is incensed by the stalwart soul that ungratefully rejects help. I was guilty of this last, most subtle form of hate towards Mrs Chambers. I was determined to prove myself capable of loving even the most repulsive of humans. But she refused to say how pleased she was to see me and how kind it was of me to come, and so I stopped going to see her. That must have caused her more unhappiness than my visiting ever caused her pleasure.

Human beings surely are naturally loving because they naturally want to be happy. But it is the existence of hate, whether overt or concealed, which stifles love. If one could gradually rid oneself of ambition, jealousy, anger, possessiveness, and the rest, the spirit of love would grow freely in their place. In other words, the art of being happy lies not so much in learning how to love, but in learning how not to hate.

I am getting around, as they say. Since leaving the chicken farm I have been a temporary butler for a pheasant-shooting party at a country house in Yorkshire, with divorced dukes and eccentric earls who doubtless went away complaining of the poor standard of domestic service these days. On the first evening I was over-generous in serving the soup — or rather the cook and I had been over-generous in serving ourselves beforehand — and by the time I reached the last guests there was barely enough to cover the hunting scene on the bottom of the plates. Dinner-table conversation was dreary, mostly about money, and the only time it became passionate was in praise of Ian Smith and his heroic stand against Wilson. I gathered that one of the party owned tobacco estates in Rhodesia.

Now I am general dogsbody at a seedy hotel behind Victoria Coach Station. It has aspirations to classiness and is decorated in royal tartan throughout, but the quality of the guests betrays it. Our most regular customer is a highly made-up lady with silvery hair, probably the wrong side of forty, who appears with a different gentleman each night. When I'm on the morning shift I serve breakfast, which is cooked by an irate Irish woman in a filthy basement. A dumbwaiter brings the undercooked eggs and burnt bacon to the dining room, but every now and again it tips up, depositing its load with a great clatter at the bottom of the shaft. The Irish cook only bothers to retrieve the cutlery and the unbroken plates, leaving the spilt food to rot. Surprisingly the smell in the kitchen is bearable. On the evening shift I serve snacks, a choice of a tomato sandwich, a cheese sandwich, or a tomato-and-cheese sandwich, made to order. I still can't chop a tomato into four slices without splattering the juice onto the wall, and I'm afraid one or two customers, having watched me make their snack, have decided to cancel their order.

As part of my wages I am given a room at the top of a Victorian house which the proprietor owns in Swiss Cottage, and an emaciated Italian lady serves me breakfast if I'm there. Since it looks exactly like the breakfast served at the hotel I have little appetite for it, and I'm living mostly on Mars bars. Still, this is fertile ground for more thoughts on the nature of happiness!

Basically there are two types of pleasure, physical and mental. A physical pleasure (or pain) is one which you have no direct control over in that its immediate cause is outside yourself. The sensation of eating good food or the sting of an insect are physical, and you attempt to control them by influencing their external cause — by buying the food, or by swatting the insect — rather than by controlling the sensation itself. Mental pleasures, on the other hand, are those whose immediate cause is, or at least can be, within your own mind: emotions, such as anger and fear, reactions to things seen or heard, and so on. In other words, mental pleasures are those where your own thoughts can control the sensation itself.

Most hateful desires are mental. I become jealous of someone because I look at him and think about him in a certain way, and if I knew how, it would be possible for me to alter my way of thinking in order to stop being jealous. Equally if I feel anger towards someone it is usually because I feel I have 'right on my side', and so presumably by abandoning my half-baked notions of right and justice I could stop my anger. Even where a hateful desire may appear to be physical, as with sexual desire when it interferes with platonic friendship, or with greed, I can perhaps learn to control it by mental discipline.

The essence, then, of learning how not to hate is:

36

1. To learn how to think in such a way as to control your mental desires so that they no longer conflict with the supreme desire to love.
2. To learn to extend the range of control, so that desires which at present are physical become mental.

I have just finished my final job of this little series, as a clerk sorting out exam papers at the City and Guilds Institute. I have been offered a place next October at Durham to study politics and philosophy, and my father has presented me with £300 with which to see the world in the meantime.

I would like to go to Australia, but judging by the cost of travel I doubt if I can get much further than India. I've booked a place on a coach to Delhi setting off in January, and I've started reading up about cow worship, the caste system, multi-armed Hindu gods, and the like. It doesn't attract me very much, but I daresay I'll enjoy it when I'm there. People keep asking me whether I'm going to India to study meditation with the Beatles and the Maharishi. I can't even sit cross-legged for two minutes without getting cramp, so I expect I would be failed as unfit before I had made my down payment.

PART 2
Wanderer

I've fallen in love. At least I think I have. Anyway I feel very happy, and I've lost my virginity into the bargain. It seems stupid, sitting here in a remote corner of eastern Turkey, but I have a great sense of victory about having had sexual intercourse. A year ago at school everyone used to brag about 'how far they had got', and of course used to lie. Something in me still wants to brag even though being at school now seems like a distant memory, but there's no one to brag to!

Belinda is not particularly pretty. When I first saw her clambering onto the coach at Brixton, with her pasty skin and mousy hair, and dressed in a King's-Road-style moth-eaten fur coat, I even felt repelled. She is five years older than I and has led a fairly grisly life up till now. She comes from a wealthy family, and since her father died has had a large income of her own. She has a house in Battersea where she has given hospitality to and slept with a steady stream of stray males passing through London. She admits that she doesn't connect sex with love, and regards sex just as an expression of friendship. When she feels especially sorry for some down-and-out chap (such as a newly-released prisoner on one occasion) she offers what she calls a 'mercy fuck', a kind of inverted prostitution. Not surprisingly she has made three suicide attempts and goes regularly to a psychiatrist. Her friends in London seem mostly to be aspiring artists, poets, pop singers (on the way down), and high-society pros. She also believes in the gospel of pot, and, on the theory that the border customs won't search anyone going towards Afghanistan rather than away from it, she has a large supply in her handbag.

But despite all this I like her very much, and though her track record wouldn't seem very promising I think she genuinely likes me a lot too. She says she regards me

41

as something different (!), and she is a very warm person. She is also intelligent and well-read, though her formal schooling was mostly concerned with horses and table manners. She is vulnerable and insecure, and liable to interpret things I say as showing that I don't really care for her much after all. It's rather unfair since she doesn't like admitting that she cares for me, and often says she just wants to give me a bit of experience. She's not sure why she's going to India. She's not interested in the meditation scene and regards all religion as phoney. But at the same time she feels India 'has something to teach her' and that somehow this trip is going to change her life. Well, she could certainly do with some changes.

Most of the other people on the coach are Australians who swear, tell dirty jokes, and refuse to accept that from Ostend onwards the natives don't speak English. To them the foreigner's apparent lack of understanding is a sign of obstinacy or crass stupidity. But there are one or two interesting characters. Brian, the owner and driver of the coach, with his cravat and cavalry twills, is intriguing for his sheer lack of morals. He is systematically working his way through all the girls on the coach, offering each undying devotion, and now seems to be landing on Belinda's friend Ann, who, with her heavy mascara and silk scarves, is the archetypal Chelsea bird. Ann claims once to have slept with Jimi Hendrix, which is an odd boast! Michael, an old school friend of Brian's, says he is on the trip to try to 'kick a heroine habit', and takes bottlesful of sleeping pills, stimulants, and pot in the attempt. Since his stated destination is Kabul chances of success seem slim. A few nights ago I had the horrifying experience of seeing him inject himself with an anaesthetic and slump instantly onto the bed with the syringe still in his arm. Fortunately Ann was still there and she 'tidied him up'.

The journey itself is fascinating, particularly since we

crossed into Turkey. Turkey is a physical place. For meals we wander down the main street of whatever town we're in, stopping at one café for spinach and yogurt, another for shish kebab, a third for sweet-meats, and a fourth for chi (tea), each course equally delicious and cheap. Then of course there are the baths, where you lie on steaming marble slabs and occasionally wander over to a fountain and douse yourself with hot water. The natural scenery here in the east is magnificent. One day we pass blood-red rivers meandering through bare, flat countryside, with blue mountains in the distance; the next day steep mountain passes, with snow sparkling purple and blue in the sun.

The only trouble is the cold. I had vaguely thought that a place like Turkey was always warm, and when I asked Brian's agent in London when I booked my ticket what I should bring he advised a sweater or two for the chilly nights. Luckily my provident mother knitted woolly socks and gloves, and stuffed a suitcase full of warm clothes, but no amount of woollies could keep out this kind of cold. The heaters on the coach, being seven or eight years old, have long since rusted up, and by nightfall there is a thick layer of ice on the inside of the windows. In the mornings a fire has to be lit under the engine to unfreeze the oil. Here in Erzurum, which is 6000 feet above sea level, it's colder than ever, and when we went out tonight to find some supper we could hardly breathe. Tomorrow we have the Tahir Pass which apparently rises to 9000 feet. So if anyone finds these few jottings frozen to a dead man's breast, shed a tear for a faint-hearted Englishman who would probably never have come if the brochure had been more honest.

Belinda now wants me to come to bed, doubtless to give me a bit more experience.

We are now stuck in a 'transport cafe' in the middle of the Afghani desert, a hundred miles out of Herat. To no one's surprise the coach's engine finally seized up and cannot be repaired. We coasted for about three miles down the side of a range of hills until we reached this mud hut in the valley, which serves rice and eggs to the handful of lorry drivers who pass each day. Once they had absorbed the ghastly truth of the situation our Australian friends fell on Brian, demanding their fares for the rest of the journey to Delhi. Brian, having deposited most of his cash with Ann, gave out what he had on him, gaily assuring them that he would refund them from his (non-existent) bank account in Delhi, and then in dribs and drabs they all hitched lifts to Kandahar, two hundred miles onwards. Now only Belinda, Ann, Brian, and myself remain.

Today is our fourth day here, and the diet of rice and eggs is beginning to pall. Brian asked one of the more friendly Australians to arrange a tow to come out from Kandahar, and all we can do is wait hopefully. Except for a few blades of grass growing by the stream, which I gather will dry up for the summer within the next fortnight, there is just bare rock stretching to the horizon. We sleep side by side with our charming Afghani café owners on the floor of the mud hut, and at night we can hear the wolves come round in search of food. When the stream does finally dry up the Afghanis will shut up shop and disappear over the hills to rejoin their nomadic kinsfolk. Apart from the lorry drivers who stop, occasionally a lone man with a camel will appear, have a meal, and continue his journey through the wilderness.

Hashish, rich and black, sometimes with opium added, keeps us amused. I am writing early in the morning because by midday I will be incapable — I will have 'freaked out', I should say. I tried opium on our first night here, sitting in the mud hut with all the Australians gabbering away, calling Brian a crook, complaining about the food, and wishing there was beer. Gradually the people around me began to look like little devils, their eyes gleaming viciously and their white teeth flashing like fangs. A brown shadow seemed to rise from their heads. Belinda herself, who had also taken opium, appeared like a pathetic little child, and as I looked into her face she seemed to be imploring an affection which I knew I could not give. Not having been warned about the wolves I went out of the hut and wandered along the stream. Then on the other side of a mound I heard wolves growling. I ran back to the hut and spent the rest of the evening shaking with fear in my pathetic Belinda's arms. Since then I've been so cautious with the amount of opium I use that it hardly has any effect.

When we grow bored with hash, rice, and eggs, there is sex, sex, and more sex. Belinda has an insatiable appetite, and at frequent intervals we go off to a cave about a mile away. My penis is now permanently sore, but Belinda prides herself on being able to add ever-new excitements to the sexual act, and I enjoy it. But I don't love Belinda; there is no substance to our relationship. If sex and hash were taken away we would just drift apart. It is easy to fall in love, and I think I did fall in love with Belinda. But falling in love isn't loving: like hashish and poetry and all the rest it is just a foretaste of the joy of love. Yet the horrible thing is that just as I am seeing through our charade Belinda is beginning to think she really does love me. She has even got to the stage of saying that when we get back to London she will seriously consider being faithful to me, and, as if it in some way ratified that assurance, she says she might apply to do an external London degree in art and history!

45

Brian has a pack of Tarot cards which he says have been a great help to him in running these coach trips. His faith in them must be boundless, as it now turns out that even if the coach hadn't seized up he wouldn't have had enough money to reach Delhi. Yesterday Brian dealt the Tarot cards for Belinda and me. I can't see quite how they work, and Brian won't explain, saying it depends mostly on intuition. The cards, aided by Brian's intuition, predict that our relationship will undergo considerable strain when we get to India. Belinda, despite her agnosticism, is convinced that this prediction contains some profound independent truth, as if it wasn't perfectly clear without the Tarot cards.

Ann, who I now realise is an utter dimwit, keeps smiling and wearing her silk scarves, and still spends three quarters of an hour doing her face every morning.

Before leaving London I had written to a school in a small town called Gulabpura in Rajasthan, on the edge of the Western Desert of India, asking for a job. Now I was sitting in the waiting-room of Ajmer Station at two o'clock at night, waiting for a connection to Gulabpura the following morning.

29 March '69

Belinda and I parted on Jaipur Station yesterday afternoon, she going to rejoin Ann in Nepal, while I head southwards in hopes of a job. We tell each other that by parting we are testing our relationship, and in the last couple of days we have grown steadily stronger and more prolific in our confessions of love for each other. Yesterday we abstained from sex, feeling that it was wrong to enjoy ourselves at a time like this. Now I can't stop crying and snivelling.

I can't stop shitting either. Ever since Afghanistan I've had the runs, and in Delhi I started shitting blood, which apparently means dysentery. Some red capsules have stopped the blood but not the runs. I am becoming used to the Indian custom of wiping your bottom by splashing water on it with your hand, and the advantage is that the buttocks don't become chafed by the continuous use of paper. To my surprise I don't mind the heat of India, though they say it's much worse before the monsoon in June, and I even enjoy the hot food.

I've just finished *Come On, Jeeves* which was on sale at the station bookstall. I've never enjoyed Wodehouse until now, and I've just worked out that by reading one Jeeves novel every ten months until I'm seventy I can finish the series. Until midnight an idiotic American hippie, dressed in red kudtah and pyjama trousers, sat in a corner of the waiting room twanging a sitar. He says there is a conspiracy, perpetrated by George Harrison

47

and Ravi Shankar, to prevent people learning the sitar by claiming it is very difficult. But, he says, a Guru in a temple in Jaipur has just taught him to play in a week, though he hopes to go back later for further tuition. His playing consisted of plucking one string in a continuous rhythm while hitting other strings at random to provide the melody. At first the other people in the waiting room found it funny but gradually grew more and more irritated as they tried to sleep. Eventually the hippie exclaimed, 'Wow, too much', put the sitar away, and fell asleep himself, since when I have been transported to a Wodehouse Utopia of the Drones Club and English country homes.

I don't like India. The filthy streets, the cripples and beggars, the crowding and the noise, the endless bland conversations with polite strangers: 'Where are you coming from? How many brothers and sisters are you having? What is your purpose in coming to our great country? etc., etc.' I haven't yet travelled third class in the trains, where the compartments look like animal boxes and are so crowded that people in the stations have to fight to get in, let alone find a seat. But judging by the state of my finances I shall have to initiate myself tomorrow. I have enjoyed the 'sights' I have seen so far, though. The Taj Mahal is very beautiful, though not nearly as large and magnificent as I had imagined. And Jaipur, built by Indian architects trained in Renaissance Italy, is fascinating, though it hardly fits the description as 'the Paris of India' in the tourist office brochure.

I expect that in a few days' time I shall begin to feel lonely. But just at the moment I feel a sense of relief to be without Belinda. What a relief to have no sex! Do I love her? One part of me says I do, and as I write I have started crying again. But whether I do or not I know that our relationship is finished. The other day she said that when we were back in London I would have some strong competition from a chap called John Barton, who apparently writes pop songs and is now living at her house in Battersea. Well, John can have her.

I've decided to give up hash while I'm in India. It's more expensive here, and anyway if I'm to appreciate India I had better have a clear head. Roll on the morning.

I am now squatting in a schoolroom in a village at the foot of the Nilgiri Mountains in the far south of India. How I have managed to get here still astounds me. When I arrived at the school in Gulabpura I found that they were about to break up for the summer holidays, and the headmaster couldn't offer me a job until the end of June. There is a V.S.O. teacher already at the school and I stayed with him for about ten days. I was introduced to and had tea with everyone in the town who spoke a smattering of English as well as a few who didn't, and in the process discovered that a number of them were disciples of a sect of wandering monks called the Terepanthi Jains. These monks came from Rajasthan but were now thought to be in the Nilgiris, 1500 miles to the south. 'So why don't you catch a train and go and see them?' asked a shopkeeper. And, having no other plans, that is exactly what I have done.

The train journey took three days and nights in a crowded unreserved compartment, sleeping on newspapers laid out on the floor at night, and either standing or squatting during the day. I had no food with me and ate only the bananas and hard savoury biscuits the peasant women sell on the stations. When I reached Ootacmund at the top of the Nilgiris I had a huge meal and a bath in a local hotel, and was told that the Jain monks had left only that morning. I hitched a lift by land-rover and caught up with them just before dusk. I have now been walking alongside them for three days, and my legs are aching and my two little toes which rub against the side of my desert boots have doubled in size. I realise how unfit I am after three months in coaches and trains.

The monks despite their hard life have on the whole made me welcome, and it is fascinating to observe their way of life. They wear only a white cotton loincloth and another strip of white cotton over their shoulders. Except for the younger ones they all have shiny bald heads (is this some Yogic trick? They have no bristles on their scalps — their hair seems just to have died), and wear a white mask over their mouths to prevent them swallowing small insects, as they believe in absolute non-violence to all living creatures. Their only possessions are a bowl for food, a strip of muslin to strain their drinking water, and a soft brush to sweep insects aside when they walk at night. Except during the rainy season they are not allowed to stay in one place for more than three days and generally move on after only a night.

Jains, according to the booklet which one of the lay followers has given me, are a small sect started by a man named Mahavir in about 500 s.c., roughly a contemporary of the Buddha. The original Jains believed in possessing absolutely nothing, and consequently (though the booklet is slightly ambiguous on this point) were nude. At some stage, however, a group of Jains were seized with Miltonic shame and started wearing loincloths; hence the first major schism. The Terepanthis are a small sub-sect of the loincloth-wearing group, and were founded in the last century as a revivalist reaction against the moral corruption then prevalent among Jain monks. The nude Jains, alas, were declared illegal by the British Raj and have now ceased to exist. The most fascinating thing about the Jains, for me at least, is their professed atheism. They believe that there is no external God, and that the aim of each man's life is by his own efforts to become perfect and so to be a god himself. The word 'Terepanthi' apparently means 'the way of becoming a god'.

Yesterday evening I was taken to be formally introduced to the leader of the monks, called Acharya Tulsi. One of the lay disciples led me into the mud hut where he was sitting and instructed me to prostrate myself before him. I managed a shallow bow before pride prevented me going further, while the disciple fell flat on his face beside me. Fortunately Acharya Tulsi just laughed. He is aged about sixty, and while most of the other monks are extremely skinny he has quite a paunch. He speaks no English and the disciple acted as interpreter. The Acharya asked me if I wanted to become a monk (I said I wasn't sure), and he then lifted up one leg and showed me the sole of his foot. The skin was hard and leathery and cracked at the edges. 'It is many miles to perfection', he said, and burst into loud guffaws. I smiled limply and the Acharya nodded to the disciple to lead me out. I'm afraid I must have seemed rather a fool, and I hope he'll let me stay.

The monks rise each morning at four and have two hours of silent meditation. Then as soon as it is light they start walking, and continue until about ten o'clock. The younger monks go off to nearby villages and beg for food. There is a rule that they should not take food which has been specifically prepared for them, but since most villagers clearly know in advance of their arrival I imagine that the women put an extra spoon in the rice pot for the monks. The monks take back all the food to the Acharya who distributes it as he thinks fit, which may explain his paunch. This, however, is their only meal of the day, and I am told that some of the older monks only eat every other day.

After the meal they have a bath and wash one of their strips of cloth (so each strip is washed every two days) and pass the hottest period of the day teaching disciples or reading, while their cloth dries in the sun. Then at three they set off again and walk until dusk. Their route is planned in advance by a lay disciple, and huts and schoolrooms have generally already been set aside in the village where they spend the night. At seven o'clock they gather for prayers, and one of the monks who has a pure tenor voice sings some beautiful ancient chants, to which the other monks growl responses. After prayers the Acharya generally preaches a sermon to the villagers, exhorting them to give up alcohol, fornication, bribery, steeling, and above all, eating meat, since the slaughter of animals amounts to murder in the Jains' eyes. If, he says, you can learn to live by these rules, then in your next incarnation you may have reached a sufficient state of holiness to become a monk!

I doubt if the ordinary villager, with hoe in hand and a family to feed, is much inspired by the prospect of becoming a monk in his next incarnation, but among those who are followers of the Terepanthi Jains by caste and upbringing there is a high degree of devotion. It is a very small sect, and apart from the thirty monks here there are only apparently ten or fifteen others wandering in other parts of India. Yet there are at least forty lay followers travelling with the monks at the moment, and they say it is common for lay followers to spend at least a fortnight each year with the monks in whatever part of the country they happen to be. The Jains are the Jews of India since by tradition they are merchants, and some of the richer, more portly disciples follow the monks in their limousines. But most who have limited means go on foot, and a lorry paid for by the rich disciples carries food for these poorer ones. Fortunately I have been classed as a poor disciple and am given the twice-daily ration of chappatti and dahl (bread and lentils) from the lorry. Interestingly enough, however, I am also treated as of low caste and therefore 'unclean', and a special plate is provided for me which is kept separate from the others.

The six hours or so of each day which are spent walking are for meditation, and strict silence is kept. This should suit me as I have always found walking an ideal context for thinking. But on the first day while we were walking through the Nilgiri game reserve the excitement of looking for monkeys swinging through the trees, spotted deer rustling through the undergrowth, and even an elephant on the far side of a clearing, blocked any godlike thoughts from my mind. And during these past couple of days I have been mainly absorbed in the pain of the swelling blisters on my feet. But clearly I can't expect to become a god overnight! As an embittered American hippie said to me in Delhi: 'Most people come to India expecting Nirvana in three months or bust.' Just now I'm in such agony that I feel I am going for bust.

My blisters at last are beginning to heal and my calf muscles harden up. We are now walking through hot dusty plains and even at night there is little relief from the heat. But I am gradually getting used to it, and when I am walking I find the heat curiously stimulating. The standards of personal cleanliness among both the monks and the disciples are so strict that I have to wash my shirt each day and my only pair of trousers on alternate days. I am now sitting naked except for the striped pair of baggy cotton underpants I have just bought, waiting for my clothes to dry in the sun. Y-fronts proved hopeless, and when I first took off my trousers at a village well in order to wash them the group of villagers standing by burst into helpless laughter. So I then bought two pairs of these striped pants which are quite acceptable here, but which of course would have the audience rolling in the aisles at the Whitehall Theatre. I am growing increasingly irritated at the crowds who come and watch my daily bath, but I am now sufficiently brazen to endure the adolescent hoots when I wash underneath my pants.

Far from ordering me to leave Acharya Tulsi has put me under the charge of Rup Chand, one of the two monks who speak English. I spend two hours with him each afternoon, and the idea is that I try to improve his English while he teaches me Jain philosophy. Rup Chand is young and still has a few hairs left on his head, and like many of the other monks is very handsome with a beautifully clear complexion. He laboriously writes down on odd scraps of paper any English words I use which he doesn't know. He takes the monastic rules very seriously, and when on the second day I bought him an exercise book to use, he immediately asked, 'Did you buy that specifically for me?' When I replied that I had, he

C

refused to take it, but said he would be most grateful if I could collect up for him any scraps of waste paper. So I now rip out a couple of the pages of the exercise book each day for him. I doubt if his English is really being improved since most of our time together is spent in silence. After each little piece of philosophy he utters I have to sit and meditate upon it, and then either ask him for the next piece or put a question.

So far Rup Chand's teaching has been centred round the five great vows which each monk takes at his initiation. The object of the Jain monk's life is to achieve complete and utter detachment from all material things, and the five vows are all directed to this end. Lay disciples are encouraged to take thirteen smaller vows which will eventually, either in this life or in a future incarnation, give them the strength to take the five great vows. The first and most important vow is non-violence, which means to avoid causing injury to all living things. This, as I understand it, is the negative aspect of love. While I have thought that harmony with the world consists in positively trying to help others, the Jain simply says you should scrupulously avoid doing harm; hence the masks over their mouths and their soft brushes. Unfortunately the vow of non-violence applies to plant life also, though plants are considered to be of a lower order than animals or humans, and so it is not quite so bad to kill them. Thus all eating is inherently wicked, and the less you eat the better. Every Jain monk should aim eventually to die by starvation, and the last Terepanthi to do this three years ago is said to have survived sixty-one days without food before he finally expired.

The second vow is non-lying. In one respect this is just a part of non-violence since lying to someone is in most cases a harmful act. But the real significance of this vow is in the way of thinking that it is supposed to engender. To think up a lie involves devious thinking, and the Jain monk should become totally incapable of all forms of sophistry, irony, sarcasm, hyperbole, rhetoric and so on. His thoughts should be as innocent and straightforward as a child's, and therefore uncluttered and clear. I now realise that my own humorous comments are mostly based on irony, and Rup Chand greets them with an uncomprehending glare.

The third vow is non-stealing. This does not primarily refer to the actual act of stealing another person's goods, since this too would be included in the vow of non-violence. It means that you should not do anything that puts yourself in a superior position to others, nor should you be jealous of the position of others. In other words, pride, ambition, envy, and so forth are regarded as wanting to steal the good fortune of others. I suppose in Christian terms the vow of non-stealing is roughly equivalent to the virtue of humility.

The fourth vow is celibacy, which again is given a wide interpretation. First of all it means that you should not only refrain from all sexual relations, but should not even think about sexual pleasure and should avoid speaking with women until you are absolutely sure of yourself. (Rup Chand did not mention the alternative possibility of homosexuality, but though the monks live in very close quarters I have seen no signs of repressed homosexual feelings.) However, the Jains equate all other forms of bodily pleasure with sex, and the monk should also learn not to enjoy his food and should become indifferent to heat and cold.

The final vow is non-possession. Like the second and third vows this also is connected with non-violence, since anything which you possess and use for yourself is therefore denied to others. Rup Chand interprets all warfare and political conflict as arising from a lack of the spirit of non-possession, and in terms of Jain philosophy, which clearly has no place for absolute standards of justice and material equality, this is obviously true. But the main significance of this vow is psychological. The monk should have no mental attachment to particular places and material objects, and because it is recognised that such attachments can grow so easily, the monk must therefore spend his whole life wandering from village to village, begging for his food.

Having suffered and denied himself every normal pleasure, and having become totally detached, what reward does the monk receive? He has perfect freedom and infinite knowledge, Rup Chand replied. This means nothing to me, but Rup Chand refused to define it further, humbly saying that since he himself had not reached this state he could not describe it. This of course begs the question why, if he has no idea what perfect freedom means, he is dedicating his whole life to acquiring it. Because, he said, all the great sages throughout history have taught that this is the real purpose of life, and that all other goals are illusions which disappear as soon as they are reached. I lamely suggested that perfect freedom might be the same as total happiness, but Rup Chand replied that while the detached person undoubtedly is happy, his state cannot be compared to ordinary human happiness since this is necessarily limited and finite.

Why is it necessary to take formal vows and become a monk? Surely it would be possible to pursue freedom without taking vows at all? Rup Chand's answer to this was that without vows a man will continue to question the rightness of the path he has taken, and so he won't be able to concentrate fully on following that path. But when he takes vows he is in effect abandoning all doubts in order to follow the path unquestioningly. This, he admits, is a risk, but without taking this risk it is impossible for him to take more than one or two hesitant steps along the path. Rup Chand used the metaphor of a ship putting out to sea: the captain can never be sure that the winds and currents will be favourable, but unless he is prepared to trust his judgement he can never proceed further than the few yards' length of the mooring rope.

Another question I have asked Rup Chand is whether he considers he is being a burden on the poor villagers by begging food and giving nothing in return. Surely in fact by imposing themselves in this way the monks are making it more difficult for the villagers to pursue freedom. To this Rup Chand told a parable. 'There was an impatient farmer who tried to make his crops grow faster by pulling them up. A monk who happened to be passing saw this and called out, "You will never make your crops grow faster by pulling them. I have a better way. Let us sit together and meditate upon the power of the sun, and then the crops will ripen in no time." So the monk and the farmer sat down, and became so absorbed in their meditation that they remained there for an entire month. When at last they had finished the farmer found to his astonishment that his crops were ripe and ready for harvesting.' I have not felt it proper to ask Rup Chand for an interpretation of this story, but, as I understand it, it has two meanings. First, that the monk does give something in return, namely his teaching. And second, that food does not really belong to the villagers anyway since it is ripened by the sun: so by begging and depriving them of some of their food the monks teach the villagers the virtue of non-possession.

Rup Chand is very keen for me to take the thirteen small vows of the lay disciple. These are simply moral injunctions and, except in minor details, are the same as the ten commandments. Since I have never been impressed with the ten commandments (why should I honour my parents if they're not worthy of honour?), I am not tempted to take the thirteen small vows. The wisdom and profundity of the five great vows, at least as Rup Chand has explained them, are much more attractive, though of course I can't see myself actually taking them either.

We have now spent three days in Mysore City and, according to Jain rules, tomorrow we must move on. My lessons with Rup Chand have stopped for the time being, and the monks have been involved in a series of civic receptions and with uttering wise words to the stream of ordinary townspeople who come to see them. For a westerner like myself it is extraordinary to see a group of impoverished monks wandering on foot into a large city being given such a rapturous welcome. As they approached the city people rushed out to greet them and prostrate themselves before them, and onlookers cheered. Then the mayor gave a huge reception under a specially erected marquee in the municipal park, and Acharya Tulsi preached a sermon through loudspeakers to at least ten thousand people squatting on the grass. The next day there was another reception in the marquee during which a beautiful young man dressed only in a narrow loincloth took vows to become a monk. From the cheers of the crowd as Acharya Tulsi presented him with his mask, begging bowl and brush, it could have been a coronation, with the High Priest presenting a new Maharajah with crown and sceptre.

Both the monks and lay followers have been put up in the large Boys' High School, and as I write I am sitting beneath a flickering hurricane lamp in the geography room, with shadowy maps of the continents on the walls around me. As the weeks pass the weather grows hotter and somehow in a large city feels much more oppressive. The school lavatories haven't been cleaned out since we arrived, so the smell of sewage hangs in the air. We were entertained earlier this evening by an old monk called Natmal who is able to memorise long strings of numbers and sentences in any language, and to repeat them ten minutes later. I asked him to memorise the

61

phrase '*amor vincit omnia*', and embarrassed titters arose from the audience when I translated it. Natmal explained at the end, with no apparent pride or arrogance, that this memory feat is just a small piece of evidence of the god like powers which any monk naturally acquires as he follows the path of detachment.

I have made friends with a man called Ramachandran who teaches Hindi (the north Indian language) in Quilon, a town on the south-west coast, and who has been acting as translator for the monks who themselves speak none of the southern languages. Originally he became translator simply to have a free holiday during the vacations, but he now regards himself as a disciple of Acharya Tulsi. He has decided to give up alcohol, tobacco, meat-eating, and fornication and intends to take the thirteen smaller vows. He seems so innocuous that I doubt if he ever had these vices in the first place, but, like the Bible-thumping Christian who has been 'saved', it now suits him to believe that he did. Ramachandran is now like a brother to me, as he puts it, and since arriving in Mysore we have done our sightseeing together.

Yesterday we went up Charmundi, a conical hill that rises about a thousand feet out of the flat countryside to the south of the city. Numerous pilgrimages are made to Charmundi and it is apparently extremely holy, but no one we asked could explain why. We started to walk towards the hill from the city at midday, and as the sweat poured off us the hill seemed to move further away. 'Ah,' exclaimed Ramachandran sadly, 'this is why it is a hill of pilgrimages. It is like God: the nearer you approach, the further away he appears.' When at last God stopped running away from us and we reached the foot, we found rows of small stone huts for weary pilgrims to rest in awhile before making the ascent. But Ramachandran refused to rest: 'You are an Englishman and I am a mad dog in the midday sun', he cried, and started to bound up the narrow steps which have been cut into the rock.

About halfway up we came face to face with a huge statue of Nandi, the divine bull, cut out of the rock and standing about twenty feet high. His body has been blackened with charcoal but his eyes, which stand out like balls from his head, have been painted white and red; and his mouth, with a set of gleaming white teeth, has a sweet, gentle smile. Pilgrims tie garlands of flowers to his tail. A few yards away a priest who looks after him lives in a cave and regularly burns sacrifices to him. As we walked on Ramachandran explained why Hindus regard the cow as holy. The cow is a symbol of both love and patience. The cow's love is shown in her many gifts to man, for which she asks nothing in return: she yields milk, she pulls the plough, her dung is used for fuel, and when she dies her skin is made into sandals and her bones ground up to make fertiliser. At the same time whatever cruelties and insults men may inflict upon the cow, she remains calm and patient, and stares back at her tormentor with detached disdain. At the end of this lyrical explanation Ramachandran stopped, turned to face me, and said: 'Oh, my dearest brother Robert, if only you could learn from the cow. Your heart is so often filled with anger and sarcasm. Why not let it be filled with the pure white milk of the cow?' I am afraid that my reaction itself justified this remark, for I could barely stop myself from being rude and making some nasty comment in return.

At the top of the hill there is a large temple surrounded by tea shops, Coca-Cola stalls, and peasant women selling coconuts and bananas for the pilgrims to offer to the temple gods. We had a cup of tea and then went through the heavy metal doors of the temple, past the merchants selling images of Siva and Vishnu, and into the inner sanctuary. There we found a cluster of men in a close circle, and peering over them we could see a scrawny old woman, dressed in filthy rags and with tangled, unwashed hair, sitting cross-legged in their midst. She was shaking her body and head from side to side. Gradually her movements grew faster and more frenzied, the men became excited, and she started letting out cries and shrieks. This lasted for about three minutes, until she reached a loud climax and stopped. She paused for a moment, rose to her feet, and walked away. Unfortunately Ramachandran had not understood the woman's cries, but remarked that she was certainly a very holy woman. We then left the temple, had another cuppa, and descended the hill in silence. As Belinda would have said, I felt pretty freaked out.

Today we returned from the sublime to the ridiculous. The mayor of the city had offered to give the lay disciples a free tour of the Maharajah's palace. However, when we arrived there were at least three hundred people at the palace gates, all claiming to be lay disciples. The palace officials, who like me have scant respect for the cow, grew increasingly angry and started hitting people at random with their batons, until someone opened the gates and we all surged in. Sensibly we were divided into three groups, Ramachandran and myself in the first, and the official guide appeared, dressed in khaki battle dress with a red sash and carrying a rifle and bayonet. He led us at the double through the state dining room which, as I glimpsed over the heads of the crowd, appeared to be decorated entirely in peacock-blue stained glass. Then up into a ceremonial chamber with a large wooden throne in the middle, round a murky hall filled with moth-eaten lions and tigers which the previous Maharajah had shot, down a flight of stairs, and through a back entrance into the parade ground outside. The guide took off his helmet and passed it round (without much success) and then ran off to escort the next group.

For the first time since leaving London I am feeling homesick. I had a small bout on the train journey to Ootacmund, but apart from that I suppose I have been too constantly occupied. But since arriving in Mysore, and living in the midst of the filth and poverty of a big city, I have started to yearn for the peace and comfort of home. Also I still miss Belinda. Though it's only a month since we parted, she is already a fading memory, her face pictured in my mind in soft, blurred colours. Yet when I think about her my eyes still become moist and I have to blow my nose!

Pimples are starting to break out on my face. I think it is the heat and the poor diet, but Ramachandran insists it is a sign of my inner tension and anger.

Tonight we shall reach Seringapatam, which two hundred years ago was the capital of south India, but now I gather is just a small market town. Ramachandran and I have decided to leave the monks there and travel by bus to some of the 'sights' of this region. I feel that I have gained what I can from being with the monks, and Rup Chand doesn't seem to have much more philosophy to teach me.

In fact, judging from yesterday's lesson, he has abandoned philosophy altogether and is trying to break through my spiritual resistances by more subtle means. As soon as I sat down in front of him he started asking me personal questions. Did I wash my own clothes? What was my income? Had I ever eaten beef? Why had I come to India? Was I a virgin? He didn't appear to listen to my answers, and after about ten minutes of this he said: 'How useless and dull all this information is!' and announced that the lesson must now finish as someone else wanted to see him. The point he was making to me was obvious enough, but the odd thing was that as I had been coming to the lesson I had been framing in my mind tactful questions I could put to him to find out about his background and personal life. Another example, perhaps, of the godlike powers these monks are supposed to acquire!

On the day before yesterday Rup Chand introduced me to one of the very old monks called Sanpath. I was privileged to learn something of his personal life. As a young man he had married, and on the evening of his wedding he had taken his vows as a monk and his wife had entered a Jain convent. Since then they have never seen each other. So why had they married in the first place? 'Because our parents had arranged it, and they thought that by marrying us they could foil our desire for the holy life', he replied, with a slight smile. 'And, of course, we have been very happily married — in fifty years we have not had a single cross word!' He allowed himself to laugh a little. As I was leaving the young son of one of the lay disciples came up to announce that Zakir Hussain, the President of India, had just died. I remarked how sorry I was to hear it. Sanpath, to whom Rup Chand translated my remark, looked at me and laughed: 'You have much to learn, my friend. Why be sorry when a distant and decaying body disappears?' It was no use my answering that good manners and not ignorance had prompted my remark.

I have discovered the reason why all the monks are bald. On the day we left Mysore Rup Chand said that he was going to 'erase' his hair and beard that evening, and asked me if I would like to come and watch. When I arrived at the village schoolroom where the monks were staying that night Rup Chand was seated in a corner plucking out the hairs of his beard by the roots, one by one. When he saw me he stopped to explain that this is something that all the monks do twice a year, and the purpose is to teach themselves to remain calm and peaceful under physical pain. He admitted that he had not yet fully learnt to remain peaceful, and he was clearly under great stress. I stayed to watch him pluck a few more hairs and then left, not knowing quite what to think. The sight of Rup Chand's anguished face continues to haunt me.

In our attempt to see the temples and holy places of this area Ramachandran and I seem to spend most of our time in bus stations, having missed by minutes the last bus for hours to wherever we want to go. Once again cow worship wins the day, and Ramachandran's smiling tranquillity compares favourably with my festering irritation.

Tonight we are at Belur, which has a fine medieval temple whose outside walls are decorated with elaborate stone carvings depicting the Hindu myths, which Ramachandran related in laborious detail as we walked round. By chance there is a festival going on, and at dusk small stone cups protruding from the temple walls were filled with oil and lighted wicks placed in them, so that from a distance the whole building resembles a glittering chandelier. The town is crowded with visitors, and we have been lucky to get a room in a sleazy hotel near the temple.

The highlight of our trip, however, has been Sravanabelagola. This is a huge statue of a Jain saint, sixty feet high and carved from a single rock, and stands on a low granite hill remote from any town. Apparently when the Jains split over the question of wearing clothes, the nude group, who were persecuted by the more powerful clothed group, fled from their home in north India and settled here. The statue which they erected, and which is now all that remains of the nude Jains, is of one of the legendary Jain saints called Gommateshvara. Gommat was the eldest of two sons of an illustrious king. On his death-bed the king made the time-honoured mistake of dividing his kingdom into two equal parts, one for each of his sons. Naturally war broke out between the sons, but rather than condemn whole armies to the slaughter they decided to settle things by single combat. For three days and nights they fought without either son showing any signs of weakening, but at last on the fourth day Gommat knocked his brother to the ground. But as he was about to cut his brother's throat Gommat saw in a flash the folly of worldly ambitions which drive brother against brother. So he threw his sword away, lifted his brother up, and gave the entire kingdom to him. Gommat then decided to become a saint, and he climbed up a rocky hillock nearby and stood at the top quite still and meditated for two years, without eating and drinking. Creepers grew up round his legs and snakes crawled over his body. At the end of the two years his spirit was freed, and his body and the plants and snakes on it then turned to stone.

And that, believe it or not, is the origin of the statue there today. In my opinion it outdoes the Taj Mahal in sheer beauty. The body, though stylised in form, looks almost alive and breathing, and the creepers seem to cling to his firm, strong legs and round his genitals (which, perhaps naturally after two years of disuse, are disproportionately small). But the most magnificent part of him is his face, for it epitomises the Jain ideal. His eyes stare disinterestedly into the middle distance, and he is completely expressionless except for a slight smile at the edges of his mouth as he contemplates the folly and ignorance of ordinary human beings.

Since we left the Jain monks, in the idle hours in bus stations or jolting along on the rickety buses when they eventually come, I have been ruminating on the Jain ideal, and in particular on their idea of detachment. In terms of my previous thinking, it could be said that all hate stems from attachments, and that learning how not to hate is equivalent to achieving detachment. Ambition is an attachment to respect and status, jealousy is an attachment to the position or possessions of others, possessiveness is an attachment to the affection which others give you, and so on. Just as the drug addict can't think of anything until he gets his fix, so an ordinary person cannot feel peace and love for the world until he has satisfied his own attachments. And, of course, most of us are so full of attachments that as soon as one is satisfied another starts niggling.

Having rid themselves of hate, however, the Jain monks do not seem to become particularly loving. They don't show great concern for their fellow men, nor are they particularly warm or affectionate. Obviously it would be impossible for a person who is completely detached ever to wish ill for others, since, unlike the rest of us, he would be incapable of taking pleasure in another's misfortune. But the Jains show few positive signs of a desire to help others. Yet without doubt they are deeply happy and at peace with the world. Somehow, through their detachment, they acquire an inner, transcendent happiness which is unlike anything that ordinary humans experience.

More thoughts on detachment. The essence of the Jain method (and, though my knowledge of it is meagre, the Christian method as well) is self-denial. By consistently refusing to satisfy your attachments, eventually they disappear. That is why the religious way of life is so unattractive to most people. In the short run you deny yourself your ordinary pleasures and receive nothing in return. It is only in the long run that it becomes worthwhile.

To be honest, though I am fascinated by it and am increasingly convinced that it is the only way to happiness, I am frightened by the prospect of a lifetime of self-denial. I don't think that it's necessary to go to the extremes which the Jains do and to try to rid yourself of all attachments at once. It should be possible gradually to lessen your attachments, reducing the most hateful desires first and then the less hateful ones later. But at the same time I feel there is a need for limited periods of intense self-denial, such as Jesus had for forty days in the wilderness. As I have found in the past six weeks, when circumstances have forced me to forgo most normal comforts, intense self-denial brings you face to face with yourself. It is only when you deny yourself all normal pleasure that you can realise which attachments are strongest and most damaging. The tension which has built up inside me as a result of continuous travelling and which makes me so irritable and short-tempered has shown me how much I need the security of knowing where I'll sleep tonight, where the next meal is coming from, and so on. The other day I actually found myself using my fists to get onto a crowded bus, for no better reason than that our travel plans required that we get on that bus. I am sure that if you begin to overcome the attachments which reveal themselves so strongly in extreme situations, you have probably gone a long way in learning to be detached in normal situations.

Though I can see that a period of fasting alone in the wilderness could be valuable, somehow I feel that for me it would not attack the attachments which are strongest. The more I think about it, the more attracted I am by the life of the wandering beggar. The Jains cushion themselves to some extent by remaining in a large group, with devoted disciples at their feet. The Hindu monk, however, wanders from village to village on his own with no one to herald his coming, so that he does not have the security of knowing that he will be treated kindly and given food and shelter by the villagers. Though all my western sensibilities recoil at the idea, having to beg for my livelihood would attack the attachments that are most hateful in me. To have dignity, to be treated with respect, to be financially independent: these are the needs which my public-school education has driven deep into me, and which, if I follow the sort of career that is expected of me, I will spend my whole life trying to satisfy. But becoming a tramp, even for a short period, will ram home to me just how stupid those needs are.

So I have decided that when we get back to Mysore and Ramachandran catches the bus to Quilon, I will go northwards and spend a week with Rustom, a rich farmer near Bombay who has invited me to stay. Then I will set off with an exercise book, a change of socks, and five rupees in my pocket, and hope for the best.

It has just occurred to me that Jesus was really just a wandering beggar after he left his home in Nazareth!

I am alone again. Instead of being surrounded by the noise and bustle of a bus station, as I seem to have been for most of the last ten days, I am in the relative calm of the railway waiting room in Bangalore, awaiting the Bombay Express. Despite the numerous times I have needlessly been rude to him and snapped his head off, Ramachandran wept as I climbed onto the bus in Mysore to bring me here. He had nobly refused to catch the earlier bus to Quilon in order to wait with me until my bus arrived. Perhaps I should have returned the compliment by refusing to catch my bus, so that we would have been stuck there until such time as our two buses left simultaneously!

Last night we had some light relief going to visit a young Guru famed for his miracles in an ashram on the outskirts of Mysore. We found him reclining on a leopard skin recovering from a heavy meal, with dirty plates beside him and six disciples seated round. He beckoned us to prostrate ourselves before him, which I'm glad to say we both refused to do. I began to ask him a few questions about philosophy and yoga, but to each he replied that the question was irrelevant. Then one of the disciples seated behind us started to wail, and we turned to look. At that moment all the disciples gasped and prostrated themselves. We turned back and saw the Guru holding a string of shiny black beads. 'Did you not see our Guru produce those beads from thin air?' one of the disciples asked. 'It was a miracle from God.'

The Guru was clearly disappointed at our scepticism. So he stamped on the ground and with a flourish of his arm picked up a lump of crystal sugar from beneath his foot. Again the disciples gasped and prostrated themselves. Then he rubbed his hands together and produced a small image of Krishna. 'Surely you are now convinced that our Guru is truly a friend of God?' asked the disciple. I replied that I would only be convinced if he performed a miracle of my own choosing – to produce a pint bottle of English milk. The Guru cast his head back and guffawed with laughter. 'You have the right mind for yoga study', he exclaimed. 'Come and live at the ashram, and I will teach you the art of meditation.' I gratefully declined and our interview ended. Is he a wise man or a trickster? Do the disciples really believe in those miracles, or are they just feeds in the act? Even Ramachandran couldn't make up his mind.

The same question arose today over two families of beggars in Mysore City. The first was in the main bazaar, and it was the most horrifying sight I have seen in India. A young boy aged about twelve was lying on the pavement with his stomach cut open and his entrails hanging out. An older lad, who was perhaps his brother, stood beside him pointing to the boy's stomach and begging for money. I could not bear to look, and I said to Ramachandran that we should call an ambulance at once. 'It's no good', he answered. 'They have cut open the boy's stomach on purpose in order to make money, and they will pick up the boy and run away as soon as they see an ambulance.' So we just walked on.

The second was in the bus station. A young mother dressed in rags and her four children were playing a kind of hop-scotch. Their few possessions – cooking utensils and strips of blanket – were stacked up on a bench nearby. For a few minutes I stood at a distance watching them. Whenever they saw a rich-looking person one of the children would run up to him and ask for money. If the man refused and waved them away, the child would not persist but would run back to his mother, and they would continue laughing and playing. Eventually they spotted me, and the youngest child ran across, looked up with a cheeky grin, and held out his hand. For some reason I wouldn't give him anything, and his poor little face crossed with disappointment and he scampered back. Ramachandran frowned severely at me, went over to the mother, bowed to her and handed her one rupee. She gave a broad smile, baring her black, rotten teeth, and returned the bow.

In India, I begin to think, nothing is quite what it seems. But then I am not what I seem. In a week or two I shall be begging for husks of bread, and I shall not really be a beggar nor a holy man. Then after that I shall be a schoolteacher, looked up to as a man of learning, and yet my only qualification is A-levels. But no one here objects to pretence and deception, and for the purposes of normal behaviour outward appearances are what matter. The man dressed in saffron will be treated as holy; the man in white shirt and trousers as educated; the man in dhoti and kudtah as an illiterate peasant; the family in rags as good-for-nothing layabouts. Yet, though the incongruity disturbs me, an Indian would readily acknowledge, as Ramachandran did, that the mother and four children in the bus station may in reality be the saints.

At last, after an impatient stay in a luxurious farmhouse near Bombay, I have begun: I am a tramp in a strange land. I have felt very apprehensive during the past week, and even now as I contemplate what I am doing I am a bit frightened.

I have decided to make my walk into a kind of pilgrimage as well. This morning I started at Ellora, the fabulous cave temples cut out of the rock cliffs by monks 1500 years ago. I shall go on to Ajanta, where there are more cave temples, and then to Mandu, the capital of one of the early Muslim empires in India. From my map I estimate it to be about three hundred miles in total. The monsoon is apparently late this year so I should complete the journey before it starts. But unfortunately I have picked the hottest time of the year, with the temperature rising to 115 degrees and the land scorched and hard. This is also the season of famine, when the villagers are finishing off last year's grain and are awaiting the rains to sow more. Rustom, my rich farmer friend, has taught me some basic words of Marathi, the local language. He has also persuaded me to compromise my original plan, and I have fifty instead of five rupees with me, so that even if the villagers will not give me food I can buy it from them.

However, judging by the welcome I have received in this tiny village, that should not be necessary. I was beginning to feel scared as night fell, and looking across the dusty plains I couldn't see even a single hut. But then I suddenly found myself walking into this village, entirely built of mud and therefore invisible in the twilight. I was taken to the village headman who has given me his own rope bed to sleep on while he will sleep on the ground beside me. I was allowed half a bucket of their precious supplies of water for a bath, and, amidst many apologies, the headman's wife brought in a hunk of hard, dry bread and a small bowl of lentils for my supper. I wasn't very hungry, but I manfully ground my teeth through the bread. Now the headman has generously lit his hurricane lamp so that I can write this. But rather than use up any more of his valuable paraffin, I must stop and earn my keep by singing some English songs to the villagers.

I can no longer feel my feet. The soles are numb from plodding, and my little toes, which are raw from rubbing against the sides of my Bombay-made plimsolls, have thankfully gone dead. My eyes ache from the sun, but it hardly matters whether I see or not. All I can concentrate on is the dull rhythm of my own plodding. I may as well be walking through a tunnel. The day before yesterday I went round the cave temples at Ajanta, which is supposed to be one of the most beautiful sights in the world, with unique wall paintings. Now I can hardly remember what I saw. Every now and again as I walk I find myself bursting into tears for no reason. Yet I don't feel sad or depressed as I cry — all emotion has drained from me. I've also started talking to myself.

Last night my spare pair of socks was stolen as it was hanging to dry. What do they want socks for? No one here wears shoes, let alone socks. When I woke up I started shouting at the man who had put me up for the night, accusing him of stealing them. Of course he couldn't understand what I was saying, and was so offended at my ingratitude that he and his brother lifted me up by the shoulders and literally threw me out of their village.

O God! How can I be such a bastard? At every village where I have stopped I have been given hospitality. They feed me supper out of their own mouths and let me have their own beds to sleep on. The couple of times I have offered them a rupee as I left in the morning it has been politely refused, even though these people are on the verge of starvation. Yet I am rude in return. I become angry when the children watch me bathe, though I am using their own drinking water just to clean my body. I glare at them when they laugh at my toothbrush. I refuse to eat when they all crowd round to stare. Why do they put up with me? Why don't they all just pick me up and throw me out?

The one thing that doesn't bother me is the heat. In fact I like it. I'm only worried about getting heat stroke. After three or four miles' walking my body has completely dried out, and when I reach a village the first couple of pints of water I drink go straight through me, and sweat pours off my body. Today I walked ten miles without water as the road passed through no villages, and by the end my mouth and body were so dry I could hardly breathe. Why on earth didn't I bring a plastic water bottle?

What am I doing here anyway? I am trying to imitate the holy men. Yet I regard religion as an intellectual fraud — simply a psychological technique for making you feel happier. And so I am driving myself insane, risking death, walking the skin off my feet, in order to feel happier! Gor Blimey.

I feel a little more perky than I did when I last scribbled in this exercise book. I know I shouldn't think of it like this, but with less than sixty miles to go the end is in sight. This village has a small primary school, and I am staying with the teacher. He has given me his transistor radio to listen to, tuned to Radio Ceylon, and they have just played Cliff Richard's 'Summer Holiday'! For the second time since I started I have had a proper meal, with chappattis, dahl, and vegetables.

Today I had the most extraordinary meeting. Early in the morning I caught up on the road with a lonely, withered old man dressed in a sparkling white dhoti and shawl with a cap on his head. Just as I had passed him he called out, in perfect Queen's English: 'Why are you in such a hurry? Come and keep me company for a while.' He turned out to be an ex-follower of Gandhi during the independence movement, and for the past fifteen years has been wandering round India gathering support among the village people for his own rather eccentric economic philosophy. He believes that the ills of the world stem from the accumulation of wealth into the hands of the powerful, and this has only been possible since the introduction of money, which, unlike all natural assets such as grain, livestock, and so on, is imperishable. Therefore he advocates a 6% annual tax to be levied on the holders of money so that in effect it too becomes perishable.

Even with my rudimentary A-level economics I could see certain flaws in this scheme. But that wasn't the point. This old man, with his goatee beard and twinkling eyes, who like me has a European education, has walked the hot dusty roads of India as I am doing for one and a half decades. And, though he readily admits that his campaign has until now been an utter failure, he is as far as I could see completely content and at peace with the world. 'It took a thousand years for the evil of money to spread round the world, and it will take another thousand to control that evil', he said with a gentle smile. We walked together for a couple of miles until he turned off the road to take his philosophy to another small village. He said as we parted that he has outlined his philosophy in detail and answered all possible objections in a small book which he asked me to purchase when I next passed through a major city. He wrote down his name on a scrap of paper — Appa Patwardhan.*

A few hours after this encounter I had a rather odd psychological experience. I remembered that in Delhi I had changed money on the black market, as in fact I had done in most of the countries we travelled through. I was suddenly seized with guilt, and in a few minutes this little dishonest act had grown out of all proportion in my mind so that I was convinced I had committed a major crime. I decided that when I reached the next town I should go to the police station and confess, and for the following hour I turned over in my mind the words of my confession so as to make the crime seem as heinous as possible. Only in this way, I thought, could I cleanse my spirit and start afresh. Then I began to contemplate the prospect of being put in gaol, and gradually I drew things back into perspective, realising that no policeman would be in the slightest bit interested in what I had to say, let alone prosecute me.

Afterwards I just laughed at myself for being so stupid. But now I am beginning to wonder if perhaps that experience wasn't so mad after all. Though the crime itself was insignificant, I would not even dream now of changing money on the black market. To

* The book, which I later bought, is called *Chalanashuddhi* and is published by the Navajivan Publishing House in Ahmedabad. By coincidence I heard recently that Appa Patwardhan died of tuberculosis not long after I met him.

commit any act of dishonesty, however trivial, would now seem totally pointless. Even in these past two months my outlook has changed quite fundamentally, and my anguish was really surprise and horror at the sort of person I had been such a short time ago.

My host has just invited me to come out with him into the fields for the 'morning motion'. (I have written the last two paragraphs just as the sun has been rising.) I hope he doesn't want to squat near me as I don't think I can manage anything this morning. Indians are always so shocked when I explain to them that I don't have regular bowel movements and am liable to go at any time. He has promised me an omelette for breakfast when we get back. What luxury!

I have finished. What a relief! The soles of my feet are
hard and my poor little toes have developed a thick
layer of leather. Now I shall relax for a few days in the
relative cool of this beautiful place. Mandu is on a high
plateau about four miles square with a steep drop on
three of its four sides. There are still plenty of remains
of old mosques, palaces, and tombs of the Turkish con-
querors who ruled from here 600 years ago, and I shall
enjoy exploring them at leisure. Unlike Ellora and Ajanta
it is not yet a tourist spot, so that from what I have seen
so far many of the ruins are overgrown, and cows now
graze and shelter from the sun where once proud sultans
strutted. I daresay soon, when the Indian Tourist Office
decides to exploit this asset, petty government officials
will evict the cows and strut proudly in their place.

So what have I achieved? I am emotionally dead, numb
to both happiness and depression. I have discovered
once again that under stress I have an evil, nasty temper.
I have also learnt how little control I have over my own
mental workings, and, try as I might, I have not had more
than three consecutive minutes of coherent philosophical
thinking while I have been walking. At times I have
been driven almost crazy by the desire for meat, yet on
the other hand I have become indifferent to the stomach
cramps I am continually suffering. The thought of
plucking out the hairs of my beard by the roots, in my
present state of mind, no longer appalls me.

Have I learnt anything about the path to happiness?
I have tried to imitate the Jain monks (albeit for a very
limited period) and yet I am now less convinced that the
Jain monks are really happy themselves. Certainly they
are not unhappy, just as I am not unhappy now. But I
am not sure they are deeply fulfilled either. Perhaps
they simply achieve total and complete numbness to all

forms of pain. Not once can I remember Rup Chand or any of the others showing real warmth or pleasure; their strongest reaction to anything is wry humour. In a world of misery and deprivation this numbness is a considerable achievement, and their life is certainly better than that of the average peasant. But I keep thinking of Appa Patwardhan. He surely has achieved as high a degree of detachment as any of the Jains through his years of tramping round India peddling an unwanted philosophy. And yet he is also warm and jolly, laughing at himself, patting me on the back for my 'brave adventure', smiling and joking with the village children who run out to meet him. What has he got that the Jains lack?

Here in Mandu I have been taken in hand by the rather obnoxious son of the village postmaster. He claims he is shortly going to Bombay to become a film star, but in the meantime he is bent on corrupting my morals. Last night, having generously treated me to a meal at the local hotel, he took me to visit one of the tribal (that is, non-Hindu) settlements on the far side of the plateau. We went into a squat, thatched hut and were treated by the family to their home-made wine. A heated conversation then sprang up between my friend and the father, while his young daughter sat in the corner becoming increasingly agitated. My friend turned to me and said, 'You can afford five rupees, can't you?' to which I nodded, not realising what it was all about. However, when my friend related this information to the father, who clearly approved, the daughter burst into tears. The truth at last dawned on me, and, apologising as best I could to both father and daughter, I hurriedly dragged my friend out of the hut. As we walked back my friend regretted not having managed to beat the price down further – 'But she is a virgin, and virgins are more costly' – and refused to believe that I did not want to 'go with a girl' anyway. He is now firmly convinced that I am just tight-fisted.

After two or three days here I shall go and visit some of the other 'sights' of central India, and then return to Gulabpura for the beginning of term on July 1st.

I was only able to spend two months teaching at Gulabpura High School before returning to Britain. During this period, however, I had the peace and leisure to read more widely in the Indian scriptures, and also to draw my own thoughts together.

16 August '69

Most of us seek happiness through the circumstances in which we live. We continually try to adapt our circumstances — by accumulating new possessions, by getting a better job, and so on — to give ourselves greater satisfaction. The religious man, however, is quite simply someone who believes that this attempt is invariably doomed to failure. He does not deny men's ingenuity and capacity to mould their environment to suit themselves, and he may readily concede that a social order could perhaps be devised in which conflict was eradicated and all men's aspirations brought into harmony. But, he says, real happiness will not come from this. Deep and lasting happiness can only come from within each person, so that it is not circumstances which need to be altered, but ourselves.

The religious man, therefore, first of all tries to detach himself from his environment. Though he continues to feel the sensations of pain, he becomes steadily less affected by it. And though he continues to enjoy normal pleasures, he grows less dependent on them. At the same time he develops within himself a deep and peaceful joy which is quite independent of the circumstances in which he finds himself and which can persist through the worst adversity. The way of detachment, the first part of the religious life, can easily be observed by others, and the past few months have been for me one long object lesson in it. The second part, the development of interior joy, however, cannot be seen from outside because by its nature it happens inside the person. It is here, then, that the real mystery of religion lies. What is this interior joy? And how does the religious man set about achieving it?

Obviously I won't know the answer to the first question until I have achieved interior joy myself. And even then, just as the wise man in the Upanishads could only attempt to describe it by listing all the things which it is not like, I doubt if I should be able to talk about it convincingly to others. But unless I can find some answer to the second question — how do I start developing interior joy? — I am stuck.

The key surely lies in the practice of prayer and meditation, which is common to every religious tradition, and which plays such an important part in the lives of religious men. For example, at the beginning of his public life Jesus spent forty days meditating in the wilderness, and at frequent intervals afterwards he used to go off alone to pray. Similarly it was while meditating under a tree that the Buddha became enlightened — that is, he achieved complete interior joy. Through prayer and meditation the religious man tries permanently to alter his patterns of thought so that his own mind becomes itself the source of his happiness. In the past I have made a distinction between physical and mental pleasures, mental pleasures being those whose immediate cause is within your own mind. Prayer, then, is simply a technique for enjoying continuous mental pleasure. It can perhaps be compared to the ordinary activity of daydreaming. For example, nostalgic reminiscences of childhood, or idle dreams of *la dolce vita* are both, like prayer, causes of pleasure which are entirely within the mind itself and therefore independent of one's circumstances — which may be a grimy railway carriage or a drab park bench. But the difference is that while the nostalgic reverie or idle dreams will sooner or later be rudely interrupted, the pleasure which the religious man derives from prayer continues, and whatever happens around him, it cannot be broken. In other words, through prayer and meditation the religious man constructs a permanent and unbreakable daydream!

To learn how to pray I must obviously study the mental processes of those people who do pray successfully (although, as Hindus implicitly acknowledge in their doctrine of reincarnation, to complete this study is likely to take longer than a single lifetime). The outstanding common feature of all forms of prayer which I know of is that they involve some belief in a supreme entity, a God. Even the Jains, who claim to be atheist, still require disciples to believe that the perfect saint is like a god, having supreme knowledge and power. Christians, of course, direct all prayers to God. The vital significance of belief in God can be seen in the two ways in which God is generally conceived. First, He (or It) is an abstract idea representing, as the Hindus put it, 'Sat-Chit-Ananda': Truth-Understanding-Bliss. In other words, to believe in God means to believe in the possibility of attaining that level of mental control which enables you to enjoy complete interior joy or bliss. Clearly unless you have this initial belief, or unless you believe it possible to achieve a very high degree of interior joy, you will not have the necessary motivation to accept the discipline of learning how to pray.

Second, God is conceived in some concrete and attractive form, usually as a human incarnation, but sometimes as a symbol or sound ('om', for example), and a large part of prayer is taken up with meditation on this concrete form. In some way the concrete form of God must have an innate appeal, evoking at the deepest level mental processes which cause interior joy. The true Christian, for instance, must have a deep natural sympathy with Jesus, so that meditation on his

88

personality is profoundly satisfying. Similarly the Hindu who repeats his mantra for hours on end finds that all normal thought ceases and his mind turns inwards to discover its own inner resources. Thus the concrete form of God is a mental image or set of images that sets in motion the particular thought processes which lead to interior joy.

I think I can say that I already believe in the abstract God. But I have not yet found a concrete form of God which particularly suits me.

Today I went to see Belinda at her house in Battersea. It felt as though we were total strangers. She has never had a good complexion, but now it's worse than ever: white and fluffy, dotted with nasty pink pimples, and with bluish bags under her eyes. I didn't like to ask, but she certainly looks as though she has graduated from hashish onto something more potent. When I arrived back from India I found a letter from her waiting for me, full of hate and poison for not having kept in touch (which had been virtually impossible with us both moving unpredictably around a sub-continent). This morning she was a bit more friendly, but announced almost as soon as I walked through the front door that John Barton had won the day! The mysterious John Barton was still in bed upstairs.

Belinda's trip in India was something of a failure, it seems, and she and Ann flew back to London early in July. Having got stoned out of their minds in Nepal, lurched down to Ceylon to stay with some rich tea-planter friends of Ann, and seen the erotic sculptures at Khujaraho, they decided they couldn't take any more. Brian meanwhile has landed himself in gaol in Frankfurt. By some miracle of charm and fast talking he managed to borrow enough money from friends in Delhi to repair his bus, and in order to recoup his losses he arranged for a garage in Kabul to fill its false roof with hash. The garage owners, however, apparently tipped off the international police (presumably being paid for the information), and when Brian arrived at the German border he was caught. By a further miracle of charm Brian has been sentenced to only a few years.

No recent news of Michael. He was last sighted a few months ago in the Khyber Restaurant, the drug rendezvous of Kabul, but it was not reported what particular combination of depressants and stimulants he was currently taking.

PART 3

Seeker

While I was in India, at almost every town I passed through, young men would come up to me asking how they could get a place at an English university, whether any scholarships or grants were available, and how much the fare to Britain was. For them studying at an English University is a passport to a successful career and a happy life, and they would give their right arms for the opportunity.

Now here I am myself at Durham University. Like the rich man in hell I should like to go back to India and warn them off. The students here are blasé and overfed, taking for granted the luxury and privilege which is denied to most of their contemporaries in the world. They have come not from any love of learning, but because they happened to achieve high enough grades in A-level (though not quite high enough to take them to the greater privilege of Oxbridge). They have never known the crude struggle to survive which occupies the young men of India, and they are tacitly aware that a comfortable career awaits them when they emerge with their degrees. To fill the dull moments they latch onto glib left-wing causes.

I am now a part of all this, undergoing the next process in the western educational sausage machine. Yet I am worse than the other students. They at least mostly fit into the sausage skins prepared for them and pass through the machine relatively painlessly. But I am so spoiled that I reject each skin before even trying it on. Before lectures had begun I decided that I couldn't face politics and philosophy, and I looked feverishly through the prospectus for an alternative. I plumped for anthropology, hoping that witchcraft, tribal magic, and the like might divert me for the next three years. But, alas, the 'academic approach' makes even these exotic subjects mundane and boring. I am spending less and less time on anthropology, and instead sit in the library avidly reading books on religion. Yet this too fails to satisfy me. The more I read about religion, the more I feel that I am an outsider looking in, lacking any real understanding.

A few weeks ago I read the New Testament from cover to cover for the first time, and I was deeply impressed by the insight and wisdom in both the teachings of Jesus and the letters of Paul. Never before has the person of Jesus seemed alive and genuine; he has always appeared as a wise man from a fairy story. But now I could imagine him, standing perhaps on a low hill outside a poor Indian village, preaching to the underemployed peasants and children who have come along for want of anything better to do; and then to their surprise he heals the old woman with the swollen leg, the child with clouded eyes, the ugly man whose face is covered with pussy swellings. As I read the Gospels I had an almost physical desire to meet Jesus face to face, to touch and feel his body and to hear his calm, gentle voice. In Matthew, Mark, and Luke I found myself nodding in agreement at the subtle metaphors and paradoxes in which he presents his teaching, wishing that I could share them with people like Ramachandran and Rup Chand who would really appreciate them. But amidst the ambiguities and oblique mysticism of John's Gospel I realised how little I understand. 'I am going where you cannot come. . . if you knew me you would know my father too. . . if you ask anything in my name I will do it. . . the Holy Spirit will teach you everything. . . you call me "Master" and "Lord", and rightly so. . .' What does all this mean? Taken on their own these sound like the words of a pot-bellied pseudo-Guru bloated with his own importance, who never speaks straight lest his deluded disciples should rumble him. Yet Jesus quite obviously was not an imposter and would presumably only talk in riddles if there were no way of speaking clearly.

The problem is that I am searching for an Agnostic God. By culture and upbringing as well as conviction I am an agnostic, and I must lead my life only on the basis of truths which can be verified by observation and experience. Jesus, on the other hand, like most Indians today, grew up in a culture which accepted the existence of a supernatural God without question, and so in his teachings the belief in supernatural power inevitably became entangled with the essential human and earthly truths he was expressing. Therefore, if I am to learn anything from teachers like Jesus, I have continually to decode their words, translating their references to supernatural power into terms of human expereince. But this is extremely difficult. What, for example, does 'faith' mean? Is it simply such a strong conviction in an ideal that you have stopped questioning it, or does it have a deeper meaning than this? And 'grace'? Is this just a more respectable word for the essentially selfish happiness which the religious man enjoys?

To add to my depression with university life I am also now having 'woman trouble'. When I came back from India I intended to steer clear of sex, as I felt that while I am still groping to find my way in the spiritual life it would be a hindrance to have a close relationship with a girl. But now I have added insult to my own injury by allowing myself to fall for a blonde called Patty. She is attractive, easy to get on with, reasonably considerate, and has all the qualities a man would normally hope for. And what's more she seems to be falling for me. But her outlook on life — which consists of getting a good degree, working in a company for a few exciting years, and then settling down near Mum and Dad in Birmingham to have a family — barely overlaps at a single point with my own aspirations. The things which obsess me are of no interest whatsoever to her. Yet I am now going to her room almost daily, thinking about her during lectures, and even having wet dreams over her!

The one bright spot in my life is the friendship I have struck with an extraordinary fellow anthropology student called Tom. He has spent most of his life in a Trappist monastery in Scotland, and now at the age of fifty has emerged to continue his monastic life in the world. I have been amazed by his descriptions of the Trappist life which in its own way is as austere as that of the Jains. The monks sleep on straw mattresses in dormitories, have no possessions of their own, eat no meat and very little of anything else, rise at three in the morning in both winter and summer for prayers, do a full day's labour in the fields, and on top of it all maintain complete silence throughout except for a short recreation period. I never imagined that such a way of life still existed amidst the flabby cosiness of normal church life. Now as a common-or-garden student Tom lives in a cold bed-sitter, unable to afford the shillings for the gas meter, and since he receives no grant, depends entirely on what well-wishing friends give him. He reminds me of old Appa Patwardhan (who, though I only met him briefly, I still think about) because despite the loneliness and hardness of his chosen lot he is invariably cheerful, welcoming, and apparently at peace with the world.

Tom, of course, is a convinced Christian and believes in an external, supernatural God. In his words, the purpose of life is eventually to see God face to face. He doesn't, however, think that Christians have a monopoly of true religious experience, and he has read widely in Hindu, Buddhist, and Muslim literature, not simply from academic interest, but to gain inspiration in his own religious quest. It is a great relief to be able to discuss things with him, and despite his belief in God there is no fundamental chasm between us. As he said the other day, we are treading two slightly different paths leading in the same direction. When I replied that of course he was a great deal further along his path than I along mine, he said: 'It's extremely difficult to make such comparisons. The nearer you approach God, the further away you realise you are from Him — it can be very frustrating.'

The only direct piece of advice Tom has given is to quote Anselm, a medieval Archbishop of Canterbury, who said: 'I believe in order that I may understand.' According to Tom I always insist on understanding something before believing in it, with the result that I understand less than I would if I had let myself believe in it first. That seems to me a very dangerous view, since to believe in something without first understanding it fully means in effect you deliberately suspend your critical faculties.

The Christmas vacation has fortunately cooled my ardour for Patty and hers for me. Since we never confessed our passion for each other there has been no need for a parting scene, and we now just give each other an embarrassed smile when we pass in the street. Phew! But the grind of anthropology goes on. I have now discovered why it is so dull: anthropologists have an obsession with 'objectivity'. Unless they can be sure that a particular thing is objectively true, they refuse to discuss it. Thus every tribal custom and ritual is seen from the outside, from the viewpoint of the 'detached observer', and the cardinal sin for the anthropologist is to use his imagination to understand what he sees. And so he understands little.

During the vacation I read Max Mueller's book on Ramakrishna, a famous nineteenth-century religious teacher in Bengal. Though I personally feel no particular attraction to Ramakrishna, as many westerners do, he was certainly a fascinating character. To outward appearances he was a lunatic. At the age of sixteen he dropped out of his expensive school in Calcutta, announcing to his horrified parents that since the main aim of school education was to teach the pupil how to earn money it was of no use to him. He became an assistant priest at a temple, keeping the shrines clean and performing minor rituals, and he gradually became obsessed with what he called 'my Divine Mother', and would sit alone in the forest for whole days and nights praying for her to reveal herself to him. At the end of each day, as he heard the temple bell strike, he is supposed to have burst into tears, crying, 'Another day of my short life has been wasted, Mother, for I have not seen you.'

Eventually the Divine Mother did reveal herself one dark night, in the form of a gentle loving voice which told Ramakrishna to stop loving himself and his own earthly comforts. So for the next twelve years Ramakrishna, who had few enough comforts already, lived like an animal. He gave up eating at the temple and instead shared the crusts which were thrown to the dogs. Then each evening he went into the temple hall where the other priests had just eaten and licked up the crumbs and slops. At night he slept rough in ditches and under trees. His reward came finally when a wandering ascetic named Totapuri arrived at the temple. As soon as he saw him Ramakrishna asked Totapuri to become his Guru. Totapuri accepted, and Ramakrishna made a vow of total obedience to him. Within three days under Totapuri's guidance Ramakrishna attained 'enlightenment'. Totapuri then disappeared without trace, and Ramakrishna spent the rest of his life teaching others.

Perhaps Ramakrishna's apparent lunacy was in fact what Jesus called 'faith'. As soon as Ramakrishna decided that a certain course of action was right — whether it was leaving school or becoming an animal — he followed it without further hesitation or doubt. Most of us never achieve such certainty in our lives, and though we may tend to think something is right we are never prepared to commit ourselves fully to it. This caution and lack of commitment is regarded as 'prudence' and 'sanity', and as a result of it most people end life in much the same spiritual state in which they began. Ramakrishna's madness was that he threw all caution to the winds in following his own convictions, and so achieved true happiness.

But I now see that such faith, as Anselm said, must inevitably come before full understanding. The process of coming to a certain belief may involve cold, elaborate reasoning, or flights of intuition and imagination, depending on the sort of person you are. But however intelligent your reasoning or however perceptive your intuition, it is impossible to be certain of the rightness of a belief until you have put it into practice. Therefore at some point a moment of decision must be reached when you call a halt to further questioning and deliberation, and simply act. This is the 'act of faith', and it is only afterwards as you experience its effects on your life that you realise the full meaning of the belief.

Though I have never thought of it like this, the few short steps that I have so far made along the religious path have been through acts of faith. For example, before I finally set off alone on foot in India I spent two or three weeks fighting with myself, questioning my own motives and wondering whether it was worth the risk. But I can now see that by being imprudent enough to go on that walk I learnt a great deal about my own spiritual resources and weaknesses. As the life of Ramakrishna shows, living by faith involves continuous risk, both psychological and physical, but unless you are prepared to take the risks the quest for 'enlightenment' is hopeless. Perhaps the same thing can be applied to anthropology: if, even for a brief period, the anthropologist could abandon his rationalist outlook and adopt the beliefs and attitudes of the tribe he was studying, he might understand a great deal more about them!

I have fallen in love; and, as a pop song would say, this time it's for real. Tom introduced me to Sarah when he and I were arranging a trip during the Easter vacation to eastern Europe. As we had two spare seats in the car Tom suggested Sarah to fill one of them, and by Salzburg (or was it Linz?) everything was roses. Now we are living together in a tumble down miner's cottage which I bought last month from the National Coal Board for £25!

Sarah has been, and in a way still is, going through a spiritual crisis. She was brought up as a good, middle-class Christian, but after a brief religious phase in her early teens which coincided with confirmation, religion rapidly went dead on her. Only recently, however, has she begun to feel the lack of any underlying meaning or purpose to life. She still believes in an external, supernatural God and, despite what she says, I think she would still like to go back to the Christian fold. Her parents of course violently object to our living together, and she has a few residual qualms as well. But what is so special about Sarah for me is that she has an intuitive understanding of my own attitudes and searchings and, as she rightly refuses to have intellectual arguments about religion, she is able to accept my views without necessarily agreeing with them. In fact one important thing she has shown me is how pointless intellectual argument over religion often is: as the argument goes on your intellectual positions harden and you find yourselves desperately trying to put into precise words spiritual truths which at best can only be hinted at in metaphors.

Falling in love hasn't let me forget my hunger for religion. I am still avidly consuming the Oriental section of the university library to the detriment of my anthropology, and each evening I go for long, solitary walks on the moors behind our cottage. It is the idea of the Guru which grips me now. In the Hindu tradition when a man decides to dedicate himself to the pursuit of spiritual enlightenment, he sets off from home to find a suitable teacher, travelling perhaps thousands of miles in the search. In India I met a number of people, mainly older men with no family ties, who had done this. One old man in Gulabpura claimed he travelled from Kashmir to Madras and across to Bengal in his search, and eventually found his Guru in an ashram only a few miles from home! A man may in the course of his travels meet numerous holy men and question them to see if they are suitable. But when he finally decides to ask a particular person to become his Guru, and that person accepts, he will take a vow of absolute obedience to him. Ramakrishna after his own enlightenment stressed the need for a Guru. 'The Guru is the mediator, bringing Man and God together', he is quoted as saying. 'In trying to reach God a man must follow unquestioningly the instructions of one single Guru who himself knows the way to God.'

Until recently I thought it was unnecessary to have a single Guru, particularly for a modern westerner who can read widely and travel, and that it was better to pick and choose from the teachings of all the great holy men in history. But now I see that this dilettante approach is not enough, for I am learning less and less from the books I read: the more different trees I pick cherries from, the less sweet any of them tastes. In the past few days during my long walks on the moors I have thought of four compelling reasons for having a single Guru:

1. When you are sampling the teaching of many different teachers, it is extremely difficult to become sufficiently convinced of the truth of any particular teaching to

make an act of faith on it. For example, I have been impressed by the Yoga teachings of Patanjali, but I cannot be certain that this kind of practice is suitable for me to undertake the enormous discipline it requires. Only under a single teacher, who I was convinced had himself achieved enlightenment and with whom I had a deep natural sympathy, could I reasonably take the high risks and hardships which the spiritual life demands.

2. It is presumably quite possible that for any particular person there are numerous suitable Gurus in the world, and so theoretically a man could have more than one Guru. However, humans are limited in their capacity for love and devotion, so it is better to concentrate all your efforts in learning to love and trust a single teacher than diffusing them on several.

3. The instructions of a single teacher will be consistent since they are based on his own experience. However, with many teachers there are bound to be contradictions, not because the enlightenment which they have each attained is different, but because the paths by which they attained it will have varied. For example, I should imagine that the spiritual states of Ramakrishna after his enlightenment and Jesus Christ were essentially the same, though Jesus never wept for his Divine Mother and doubtless would have been horrified by Ramakrishna's animal behaviour. For a disciple, therefore, it is safer to stick to one path than to risk trying to follow lots of paths at once.

4. Religious truths very often cannot be expressed fully in words, and so you find that each teacher gives his own subtle innuendoes and slants to the words he uses, building up a kind of secret vocabulary. For instance, in Jain teaching the word 'bramacharya' which is normally translated as 'celibacy' has a whole host of implications

and shades of meaning which the English word doesn't convey. Similarly in Jesus's teaching words like 'blessed' and 'grace' cannot simply be interpreted as 'happy' and 'gift', but presumably have profound inner meanings which a non-Christian like myself cannot hope to grasp. Consequently it is far better to become immersed in the language and symbols of one particular teacher rather than grapple vainly with lots of different languages.

So if I am to progress further I must set off in search of my Guru. I can't see that I shall be losing anything by dropping out of my anthropology course since I have never properly dropped in. Sarah, who is in her second year of anthropology, is pretty fed up with it as well, and last night we decided that she will ask the department if she can take a year away, and I will announce that I am leaving for good. And as soon as term ends we'll fly to Bombay. If I find my Guru and am able to make a vow of absolute obedience to him, it will be the single great act of faith which will make possible all the subsequent acts of faith that the religious life demands.

Soon after arriving in India we met a young 'Syrian' Christian called Philippos Thomas who suggested we visit a small Christian ashram of which he was an associate member. We did so, and stayed there for the following ten months. It is the Christa Sisya Ashram, ten miles north west of Coimbatore city in south India.

17 August '70

The sun has just risen and is casting long shadows up the valley. I am sitting on the veranda of our room, having risen too late to attend dawn prayers, and a good hour and a half too early for the breakfast of millet porridge and molasses. My tummy's rumbling already.

The ashram is situated in a hot, dry valley at the foot of the Nilgiri Mountains, with steep rocky ridges on either side. The valley acts as a wind funnel, and each day from soon after midday until dusk clouds of yellow dust are swept onto us. Even hourly applications of Johnson's baby lotion can't preserve Sarah's peach complexion from such an onslaught. For some reason the valley misses completely the main summer monsoon, and has to rely on the less predictable November rains, with the result that most of the land is bare and un-cultivated. In the immediate vicinity, however, the fields are lush and green, growing rice, sugar cane, and corn, as this has been the scene of a government-backed well-digging project, and many of the farmers now have electric motors pumping water onto their crops. But this glory, it seems, will be short-lived as the water table is falling rapidly and wells are already beginning to dry up.

The ashram itself consists of a series of long, low huts made with mud bricks and woven coconut leaves, built between vegetable patches and small paddy fields. In the centre is the tiny chapel with a single white washed wall at the west end against the wind, a tiled roof for shade, and an enclosed altar. The floor is polished concrete, and as each person enters for prayers he takes a small cotton mat on which to kneel from a pile in the corner.

It was founded in 1936 by Herbert Pakenham Walsh, a retired Anglican bishop of Assam, and a group of young Syrian Christians. The Syrians are the original Christians of India, and, though they claim to have been converted by the apostle Thomas coming to India, they probably originate with an influx of Christian refugees from the Middle East in the fourth century. Over the centuries they have become integrated into the caste system, Jesus presumably being regarded as the particular caste deity, and only recently under western influence have they begun to reassert the distinctiveness of their faith. Though an ashram is essentially a Hindu institution, being a place where a Guru resides, Bishop Walsh and the Syrians wanted to establish a Christian ashram, with Jesus Christ as their Guru and the life of the ashram as an embodiment of his teaching. So they came to this valley, where at that time the impoverished people were plagued with malaria, and bought these five acres of land. They dug a well, rigged up a windmill to pump water for irrigation, and baked their own bricks to build the chapel and huts.

Bishop Walsh had in tow his astonishing wife Clare. The story is that after he had been in India some years he wrote to Clare, who was the sister of an old school-friend and whom he remembered as a sturdy and resourceful young woman, and asked her to come and join his work by marrying him. She caught the next boat to Calcutta and they were married as soon as she arrived. When he retired as bishop and started the ashram, she took on all the cooking and sewing for the members. Each year she would buy a length of khaki drill and make Bishop Walsh two pairs of Bermuda shorts and two short-sleeved shirts. For herself she would make a low-waisted twenties-style dress, and as her one extravagance wore a coloured band round her hair. The food was steamed rice and a single vegetable for lunch and supper, and Irish soda-bread for breakfast (the millet porridge we now enjoy is a later introduction). Bishop Walsh, being from the Anglo-Irish gentry, had considerable private means, but whenever the young Syrian Christians with him started weakening and yearning for better food, electric lighting, enamel toilets, and the like, he would reply that Christians should always be as poor as their poorest neighbours, since inequality is the root of envy. In one respect, however, Bishop Walsh did impose English standards on the ashram: afternoon tea was, and still is, served promptly at four. But instead of crumpets and cakes they had boiled tapioca roots!

The bishop died in 1959 and Clare two years later, and even by that time some of the original members had left to become academics, teachers, and the like. Now only one of the original community remains, and there are four other younger male members plus two pious widows who do the cooking. Without Bishop Walsh's firm hand things have slipped slightly and we now have three vegetables with our rice, and a forty-watt bulb hangs in most rooms. Yellowed and curled at the edges, the typewritten timetable of the ashram signed by the bishop is pinned up in each room: rise at 4.30; morning communion (which in the Syrian rite lasts two hours and is sung standing up throughout); meditation until breakfast at eight; community work until midday prayers (when an old missionary prayer book is used which amongst other things begs for the 'conversion of the infidel'); rest and private study after lunch until tea, and then manual work in the vegetable patches until evening prayers at dusk; supper at 7.30, followed by recreation; compline at 9, and bed at 9.30. The 'community work' which occupies the mornings apparently used to mean going to the nearby villages and giving simple medical treatment and teaching children to read. But now there is a government clinic and primary school. So instead the members are building a library and guest houses near the ashram to satisfy the increasing demand for 'retreats' among middle-class Hindus and Christians from the big cities. I am afraid the bishop's original conception of the ashram as a living embodiment of Jesus's teachings may be lost under the welter of administrative work a retreat centre will entail.

One tradition established by the bishop which has remained fully intact is joke-telling at supper. Bishop Walsh apparently had a stock of jokes which he never tired of repeating, and his long beard and huge shoulders would shake as he bellowed with laughter at each telling. These jokes are now duly repeated to all newcomers, and everyone's favourite is the one about the honeymoon couple on their wedding night aboard an ocean liner. The husband was feeling rather sick because of the rough sea and could not bring himself to be suitably romantic. The bride, on the other hand, was unperturbed by the sea and kept nudging him, saying, 'Charlie, won't you kiss me?' Eventually an irate voice came from the next door cabin: 'For heaven's sake, Charlie, kiss the woman, so we can all get some sleep.' That, at least, is the bare bones of the joke, though, as we have found from the three different members who have related it to us, it lends itself to considerable embellishment. Newcomers are then asked to offer their own jokes, but we have made rather a poor showing so far. The centipede with the wooden leg who went 'ninety-nine plonk' raised only mild titters.

The ashram members have asked us to stay and join in the work of the community. But since we are not Christians and so cannot fully share its aims and spiritual life, they have suggested we build ourselves a hut on some uncultivated land a short distance away. Whether or not we really have any contribution to make to the ashram's work, the prospect of building a hut and learning how to fend for ourselves in rural India is too good an opportunity to miss. So we are at the moment negotiating a price with the farmer who owns the land, and next week we shall go to the land registrar in Coimbatore to draw up a contract.

We have built our hut and have been installed in it now for a fortnight. Architecturally it is a scandal to the neighbourhood. Indians are obsessed with security, and even the humblest mud hut has metal bars and shutters over its tiny windows and a large padlock on the door. Our hut, however, is completely open. The mud-brick walls are only three feet high, and the space up to the roof is covered by flimsy canvas flaps. Instead of a door there is an open passage through the middle of the hut with our 'sitting room' and bedroom on either side, each measuring seven feet by six. Though all our possessions are there for the taking when we are out, so far only a couple of carrots have disappeared. A labourer came from Tadagam, the main village, to help us build it, but we did most of the work ourselves with the aid of a manual on low-cost building from the British Council Library. When we started crowds of men came to stare at us while we sweated in the hot sun sawing wood and hammering nails. Fortunately the novelty slowly wore off, and by the end only small children kept us company, and still do come to watch us cook, eat, read, and sleep. I am virtually indifferent to them, but occasionally Sarah finds she can't stand their vacant stares a minute longer and flies into a rage at them.

Recently we have made friends with a Christian convert in Tadagam called Mabel. He is working as a full-time evangelist, being paid a hundred rupees (five pounds) per month by some wealthy Christians in Coimbatore to 'reap the harvest of souls where Bishop Walsh sowed'. This of course is an implied insult to the present ashram members since it suggests that they are failing to reap the harvest, and so they tend to disparage Mabel's efforts. Mabel himself is just an ordinary peasant, brought up as a Hindu in another district, who claims that as a young man he had a vision from God telling him to become a Christian. He was taught the faith by a group of Scottish lady missionaries, and at baptism adopted the name of one of them. At some stage he married and now has seven children crammed into a small hut in the village. The boys, if I can remember rightly, are called Israel, Benjamin, Johnson, and Gabriel, and the girls Elizabeth, Ebeneezer, and Grace.

Mabel is full of fun and energy, and regularly bounds over the fields to have tea with us. He thinks of himself as an Old Testament prophet, and though balding on top has grown his hair over his shoulders and wears a large coloured shawl. He has built up a group of about twenty Christians in the villages in the eight years he has been here, but his technique for the conversion of souls is a little dubious. Whenever he hears of anyone badly sick he goes straight to his bedside and asks him to pray to Jesus for help. Perhaps through Bishop Walsh's influence (who is regarded by Hindus and Christians alike as having been a holy man) he usually encounters little resistance to this suggestion, and he teaches the sick person a short 'mantra' — 'Jesus Christ, have mercy on me' — to say over and over again to himself. If the sick person dies, then Mabel announces that such is God's will, and it was therefore right he should die. If, on the other hand, he survives and gets well again, then of course it is visible proof of the miraculous power of Jesus.

Last Sunday Mabel asked us to come to his morning service at St Luke's Church in the village. The church is a rectangular shed, white-washed on the outside and plastered with dried cow-dung on the inside walls and floor. The altar is a plain wooden cross placed on an old school desk. Unfortunately we arrived halfway through the service as the boy who was to come and fetch us had not been sent off until the service was actually beginning. When we walked in everything stopped and the congregation stood up while we were taken to special mats at the front, Sarah on the left with the women and myself on the right. Then everyone squatted down again and the service was resumed. They were saying a psalm, and Mabel would yell out one verse in a high, piercing voice and the congregation would shout out the next. At the end they all shouted 'ALLELUYA', followed by a minute of total silence. To my horror Mabel broke the silence by announcing that I would now sing a devotional song, and blushing bright scarlet I went to the altar and sang 'I Believe', an Elvis Presley ballad. Unfortunately as I was reaching the climax — 'or see the sky, then I know why I bel—' — dust caught in my throat and my voice broke into a hoarse croak. There was thunderous applause and I sat down again. The congregation then bellowed out a final rousing hymn, Mabel gave the blessing and the service ended.

Afterwards Mabel invited us for tea at the 'vicarage' opposite the church. He has covered the walls of his hut with garish pictures of Jesus and the apostles against backgrounds of monsoon sunsets, snow-capped mountains, and the like, but apart from a little altar in one corner he possesses almost no furniture. During the conversation we told him we weren't Christian, but he refused to believe this. 'All British people are Christian', he exclaimed, and though we explained that this was no longer true, he insisted that our denial of faith was just humility, and we really meant that we were poor Christians. This stubbornness on his part may have had an ulterior motive, because he then suggested to us a new scheme for the conversion of souls: that we obtain Christian Aid milk powder and grain for him to distribute to the villagers, in the hope that this would further convince them of the blessings of Christianity. Apart from being in no position to obtain the milk powder, we objected that this would be 'rice Christianity', giving people food to make them Christian. 'Oh yes,' said Mabel in perfect innocence; 'that is correct. We Christians must love the Hindu people and give them food'.

Perhaps my Guru has been under my nose all my life, though it has taken two trips to India to make me start looking there. Until coming to this ashram the idea of Jesus being my Guru, or indeed anyone's Guru, had not struck me. Such phrases as 'the Son of God' and 'God Incarnate' which are virtually meaningless to me have I suppose cluttered my conception of him, and made it impossible for me to conceive of having a direct relationship with him. Yet why can't I think of Jesus Christ just as a man, as a very wise and happy man, who may be able to show me the path to happiness?

Jesus's career as a religious teacher was in his own lifetime an utter failure, and outwardly he appears as a deluded fanatic making ludicrous claims about himself as the 'light of the world' and 'the Son of Man'. Having given up a steady job as a carpenter he becomes a tramp, begging for food and shelter, and gradually picks up a group of simple-minded followers who themselves make increasingly extravagant claims about him as the messiah and the saviour of the world. After a brief spell of popular acclaim he is arrested as a petty subversive and his followers melt instantly away. At his undignified execution he is the laughing stock of Jerusalem. Yet despite all this he remains throughout his life warm and cheerful, his teaching is practical and down to earth, and even at his death he is perfectly at peace. He laughs and jokes with strangers, be they common prostitutes or wealthy merchants, and has the moral courage to defend the outcastes of society — 'Who will cast the first stone?' He is equally at ease telling homely moral fables to men with pitchforks in their hands, and running circles round the city intellectuals, outwitting them in repartee. When finally strung up on the cross he feels no resentment towards those responsible for his death — 'they know not

116

what they do' — and seems mainly concerned with the future welfare of his mother.

Jesus summed up all his teaching in the two commandments to love: to love God and to love your neighbour. The command to love your neighbour as yourself is Jesus's path to detachment. His own life illustrates how his desire to love and serve others made him give up all the comforts of home and become a wandering ascetic, in order to teach and to heal the sick. And in his teachings he is constantly emphasising that loving others demands self-denial. Faced, for example, with poverty and hunger all around you, the law of love demands that you share your wealth with the needy, which in turn means denying yourself the pleasure wealth gives. Similarly, finding a man lying wounded in the gutter, however much of a hurry you may be in and whatever the cost to yourself, love demands that you ignore your own interests in order to help the wounded man. And since, Jesus said, the poor and needy are always with us, love will always lead to detachment.

The great attraction of the law of love, however, above all the other religious teachings I have studied, is that it is a pleasurable path of detachment. Loving others is both a pleasure in itself and a means of self-denial, and Jesus constantly reiterated this. He tells his followers to 'be glad and happy' for 'happy are the merciful . . . happy are those who work for peace among men . . . happy are the poor in spirit' and so on. He himself clearly enjoyed his own service to others, his healing and teaching, and he welcomed chance meetings with corrupt tax collectors, prostitutes, and the like. Jesus rejected the rigid rules of behaviour of the traditional Jewish teachers, and no doubt would have rejected the grim vows of the Jains, the strict eightfold path of the Buddha, and even the eccentric disciplines of Ramakrishna. Instead he left it to every individual to interpret the law of love in the particular circumstances of his life, and the bulk of his teaching consists of practical illustrations and anecdotes on what love meant in certain contemporary situations.

The source of the interior joy which the religious man ultimately seeks is contained in the command to love God. Loving God is synonymous with prayer and meditation, and it is through prayer that lasting happiness is achieved. But this of course is where my understanding is so minimal, and as I read the Gospels I have to skate over the references to prayer and the kingdom of heaven. In some way, however, loving your neighbour and learning to pray are intimately related: 'The second commandment is like the first.' Whereas in, say, Jain teaching becoming detached is simply a prerequisite for acquiring interior joy, in Jesus's teaching detachment through love of neighbour actually helps you to learn to pray.

I have decided to try an experiment: to make Jesus my Guru for a test period of six months. During this time I shall act as a full disciple, studying his teachings closely and following them as far as I can, regardless of whether I fully understand or agree with them. Then on June 25th next year I shall stand back and review what has happened to me. I realise that most people would say that the act of faith in becoming a disciple of Jesus, or the disciple of any other Guru, must from the start be intended to last your whole life. If they are right my experiment will fail. But I can see no reason why a temporary act of faith can't be as strong and binding for the period in which it holds as a lifelong commitment. So I hope that during the next six months I shall at least taste the interior joy of 'loving God'.

When the idea of this experiment struck me a few weeks ago, the question of the historical accuracy of the Gospels seemed at first to rule it out. To make Jesus your Guru is not, of course, to believe in a set of disembodied teachings on the pages of a book, but is to believe primarily in the human being who teaches and whose own attainment of interior joy validates his teachings. Yet it is impossible to prove two thousand years later that the picture of Jesus in the Gospels is historically true; I have read enough fantastic accounts of Indian Gurus only recently dead to realise how starry-eyed disciples can embroider the truth. But I now feel that this doesn't really matter. Even if Jesus never existed and is entirely the product of some fiction-writer's imagination, he is still a real human figure to me as I read about him. Moreover, in order to be able to portray a man like Jesus Christ this hypothetical fiction-writer must himself have attained enlightenment, and so by believing in Jesus Christ I would in effect be believing in someone equally worthy of my obedience.

A further intellectual difficulty is what to make of the supernatural events in Jesus's life — the virgin birth, the resurrection, and so on. Without an act of intellectual dishonesty to accompany my act of faith I cannot accept these as historical, and they have all the signs of being the embellishments of later disciples. I shall therefore ignore them, except perhaps to regard them as poetic expressions of religious truths. The only exceptions are the healing miracles which I find perfectly plausible: it is to me much less extraordinary that the power of love in a man like Jesus can cure diseases than that a green mould called penicillin can.

My experiment is of course beginning on an auspicious day. Yesterday evening we went to a nativity play at Mabel's church. He had gathered together at least forty children, Hindu and Christian, to take part, and hordes of angels in dirty white shawls and shepherds in even dirtier shawls trooped in to sing Tamil carols. A real live baby plonked inside a Brittania Biscuit cardboard box played the part of Jesus, and the church was crammed, with faces peering in at every window to see the spectacle. The highlight for us was when Mabel's own children sang a special 'English Carol' which they had composed themselves in our honour, which went:

> Jacob, -acob, -acob, -acob;
> Abra-, Abra-, Abra-ham;
> Mary, -ary, -ary, -ary;
> And the Little Lamb.

This morning the village postmaster came over to ask for a Christmas tip. But since we collect our mail from Coimbatore Post Office we refused him, and after accusing us of various un-Christian qualities he stumped angrily away. At midday we shall catch the bus into Coimbatore to have a chicken dinner with the Anglo-Indian headmaster of the high school.

Sarah will for the time being remain a detached observer of my experiment, and as a lapsed Christian herself will be able to spot me trying to cheat. My most dangerous tendency will be to rationalise Jesus's instructions to suit my own preconceived ideas. Since I began to study Indian religions two years ago I am afraid I have become expert at explaining away awkward religious texts by interpreting them allegorically. I have acquired this technique mainly from the European-orientated Indian Gurus who fly round the world giving pre-digested spiritual instruction to western agnostics. Now, as a disciple of Guru Jesus, I must be more hard-headed.

Each night before going to bed I kneel for about five minutes on the ground outside our hut and slowly say the Lord's Prayer, stopping after each phrase and meditating on it. With only the buzzing of insects and the occasional shout or gale of hoarse laughter from the hamlet quarter of a mile away to break the stillness, it is a wonderfully peaceful experience, and I find I am stretching it out longer night by night.

The phrase which means most to me is 'Thy Kingdom come'. Hindu Gurus often quote approvingly from the Gospels 'the Kingdom of Heaven is within you' since this fits in nicely with the Hindu philosophy of Atman — that each person's soul is in essence identical with the Absolute. So when I meditate on 'Thy Kingdom come' I think of the interior joy which I hope one day to discover within me, and the inclusion of this phrase in his central prayer is Jesus's assurance that I can discover it. The next phrase, 'thy will be done, on earth as it is in Heaven', evokes images of a world in which all men truly love one another, and the Kingdom of Heaven spreads freely among them. This perhaps is one of the connections between love of neighbour and love of God: love between people is the means by which the belief in interior joy spreads. 'Forgive us our trespasses, as we forgive those who trespass against us' indicates another connection, that the outward peace we gain by being reconciled to one another is essential for attaining peace within. I am beginning to see that forgiveness, holding nothing against other people and having no ill feelings, is the most difficult part of love, and actually 'doing good' is easy by comparison. Two phrases of the Lord's Prayer, however, still stick in my gullet: 'give us this day our daily bread' and 'lead us not into temptation'. It seems to me wrong to ask for your daily bread, since detachment means that you should be indifferent to whether you receive it or not. Being led into temptation and being tested to discover your weaknesses and strengths is surely a useful experience. But I am now a disciple of Jesus, and though I may not agree with or understand these phrases, I still try to say them in all sincerity and hope that their true meaning will soon become clear.

We have just had a fascinating old hippie to stay with us called Ronald Rose. We heard of him through some Anglican missionaries and wrote to him a few weeks ago suggesting that he call to see us when he was next passing Coimbatore. To our surprise last week we suddenly spotted him hobbling across the fields, dressed in a faded red gown and sandals. From a minor public school and a failed novitiate in a Cistercian monastery, he originally came to India after the war to tutor a Maharajah's son in the rudiments of English and Latin grammar, and he has been here ever since, wandering aimlessly round the country from ashram to ashram. He is tall and emaciated, and has long yellowy-white hair and a shaggy beard. He peers through an old pair of tortoise-shell spectacles held miraculously together with sellotape — 'I bought them in Knightsbridge, actually.' He is a mine of hilarious stories about eccentric and perverted Hindu holy men, and has sat quizzically at the feet of almost every Guru in India. But despite the plethora of wise words he has heard he remains restless and unsatisfied. Through his whole life he has been gripped by religion, he has tried to learn more and more about the spiritual life, and yet he has never been prepared to take a deep breath, swallow his scepticism, and make the act of faith.

At one time during his monastic interlude he was a convinced Christian. But he claims that his particular stumbling-block was the doctrine of redemption, that the death of Jesus in some magical way wiped man's slate clean. Apart from being an incredible idea anyway, Ronald points out that there is no evidence that people on becoming Christians do in fact have the experience of being wiped clean; rather they become more acutely aware of their sinfulness. I cannot see, though, why believing in the doctrine of the redemption is an intrinsic part of being a Christian. Surely you can interpret the death and resurrection of Jesus as symbolising the central paradox of religion whereby the suffering involved in becoming detached in fact leads to far greater happiness. This idea, however, would not satisfy Ronald. 'When you learn a bit more about Christianity you will find that you cannot maintain the Christian faith without accepting the redemption', he pronounced.

Ronald is able to be a hippie because he has a small inherited income. But with inflation increasing and his income gradually dwindling he faces destitution within the next few years. He comforts himself with the thought that he will probably be dead before then, but if not he reckons he can keep body and soul together by becoming a third-rate Guru himself. 'I tried it before, as a matter of fact, in a temple in Lucknow. I never hit big, but I was given enough by young American travellers to see me through until my next cheque arrived from London.'

As I try to follow Jesus's instructions my agnosticism is beginning to waver. When I am angry or depressed or in any other unloving mood, I make myself say little prayers asking for help to overcome the mood. I do this because Jesus instructs me to, and for the purposes of the prayer I conjure up in my mind an image of a loving father who is able to help me. To my surprise, however, I am generally finding the prayer works, and my bad mood quickly disappears. To give a typical example, the other night I became very irritated with Sarah over a series of trivial domestic mishaps (many of which were my fault, of course) and usually in the past a black cloud would have hung over us for the rest of the evening. But on this occasion I went out for a short walk and prayed to my imaginary loving father, and by the time I returned the irritation had gone completely.

I realise that there could easily be some natural psychological explanation for these experiences. But what leads me to think that this is not the case is that I also have the strong impression of an outside force working within me. It seems to demand my submission, and having submitted to it I feel I have no control over it. Two or three times I have had the fleeting sensation of standing outside myself and watching my own mind and emotions being manipulated. I am also now aware of the force each evening as I say the Lord's Prayer when I reach the phrase 'thy will be done'. As I turn the phrase over in my mind I sense the presence of a will greater than my own, pressing upon me. Sometimes this presence becomes so strong that I can almost feel it draw close to me in the darkness, as if the warm night air was suddenly heavy and humid.

Sarah remains sceptical.

This morning I received Communion for the first time. We are staying at Tirupatur, another Christian ashram about a hundred miles southwest of Madras, and the church, built about forty years ago, is in the style of an ancient south Indian temple. The service which we attended was mainly for the Christian converts from the surrounding villages, and I knelt on the stone step to receive the bread and the wine next to the old blind weaver who makes the cloth for the ashram members. On the altar there is a bas-relief sculpture of the cross standing on the lotus flower, symbolising Christianity as the fulfilment of the Hindu religion, just as it is the fulfilment of Judaism.

No one knew that this was my first Communion, and strictly, since I am not confirmed, I should not have received it. But I did so in obedience to Jesus's command, 'Do this as often as you remember me', and of course the setting could not have been more appropriate since I have become a follower of Christ by way of Hinduism. I was a little nervous when I received the bread, and I think I half expected some special feeling to come over me as I swallowed it. But it was only afterwards during the period of silence that I realised the full meaning of what I had done: that in a single act I have proclaimed my oneness not only with Jesus Christ himself, but with all his other followers in the world, be they humble weavers in India or pin-striped members of the British Conservative Party. As a disciple of Jesus I am now bound in love to people I loathe! This was the first time that Sarah had received Communion since her pubescent religious phase, and though I would like to have received it next to her, custom demanded that she receive it with the women after all the men had returned to their places.

The priest who took the service, called Kurian, has been detailed to look after us during our stay here, taking us round the villages and showing us the various good works which the ashram is doing: caring for advanced TB cases in an isolated hamlet, and running a small primary school and clinic. Kurian is an ex-merchant seaman, and for the past few years has been living alone as an evangelist among tribal people in the mountains. Unfortunately he had to leave because, as he told us with tears in his eyes, he fell into the snares of lust. But after a few months here living on dry bread and rice cakes to cool his ardour he intends to return. This afternoon he took us to the clinic to show us a young woman who has apparently been cured of some fatal disease by a faith-healing service he conducted last week. The woman seems very placid and ordinary, but Kurian described how she screamed and tore at her hair as the evil spirit departed from her. In India one meets at every turn stories of miracles — levitations, fantastic cures, and even yogis rising from the dead — and often it is perfectly clear that the miracle has occurred entirely in the imagination of the teller. And yet Jesus not only performed such miracles himself but also taught that if we have faith in God's power we should expect to be able to perform them ourselves. So perhaps every Christian should regard it as an essential obligation of his discipleship to try to heal the sick in this way. A far cry from the timid Anglicanism of my forefathers!

A further conundrum I am struggling with is the question of the afterlife. Jesus seems quite specific that there is life after death — or rather that there is 'eternal life' which may be a different thing — and that one's main purpose should be happiness then rather than now. Not only does the idea of an afterlife go strongly against my intellectual grain, but also it frightens me. Christians, I know, generally claim to be comforted by the thought of life after death, but I would rather believe that utter oblivion, without fears and worries, awaits me in the grave. Yet, as Jesus teaches that there is eternal life, I must try to believe it and if possible understand something of what it means. Perhaps, as poets and romantic novelists say, there is some eternal quality in love. A fully loving and enlightened person has a constant and unchanging joy, whatever he is doing and whatever happens to him, and something which is changeless appears to be everlasting. Buddhists in fact equate changelessness with infinity, and they explicitly seek to achieve a state of utter changelessness.

As I write I am amazed at how quickly my experiment in faith is altering my outlook. Two months ago I wouldn't have dreamt I could think seriously about the notion of life after death and the existence of a supernatural force manipulating men's minds and curing diseases. I wonder what other old wives' tales I shall believe in before June 25th!

I hardly think I need wait the full six months. I am already firmly nailed to the cross of Jesus and am enjoying it enormously. I feel at the moment as though I am falling in love with Jesus. At the beginning of my experiment he was simply a wise teacher who had impressed me deeply. But now, just as a likeable but quite ordinary girl appears to her lover as Miss World, the image of Jesus now excites and thrills me, and I am overwhelmed by his sheer beauty. I have consciously refused to form any physical pre-Raphaelite picture of Jesus in my mind — the dewy-eyed portraits of Jesus beloved of Indian Christians positively repel me — and yet his attraction for me is almost physical in its expression. As I read the Gospels I can hear his gentle, firm voice and see the sweat-sodden cloak clinging to his lean, fragile figure. And during my nightly prayers, alone in the darkness, I find myself yearning to feel his warm, moist breath on my face. As the Book of Revelation says, he is the bridegroom and we are his brides!

I was a little worried about my feelings towards Jesus until a week or so ago when I was reading the story of the Transfiguration, and I realised that my own experience resembles that of Peter, James, and John on the mountain. Suddenly before their eyes their leader, the wise carpenter from Nazareth, became a shining hero, 'his face as bright as the sun, and his clothes as white as light'. At that moment they fell in love with Jesus and they threw themselves down at his feet in total submission to him.

In my prayers I feel the presence of the supernatural force (I am embarrassed to use the word God after so many years of agnosticism, but from now on I must compel myself) ever more strongly. It's becoming almost a matter of habit now to turn to God in prayer at frequent intervals through the day, asking for help and guidance. For most of the last six weeks we have been travelling, spending whole days and nights in crowded third-class railway compartments or sitting three to a seat on bone-shaking buses, and in the past I would have become increasingly irritable and rude to people. But this time I find I only need to immerse myself in prayer for a minute or two and my irritation and ill feelings disappear. Though I admit I have lost my temper once or twice with stubborn railway guards and the like, I am a docile angel compared to my usual self. I even find myself welcoming those interminable 'Where are you coming from? What is your income?' conversations with blank strangers, returning fire to elicit the same information from them.

Sarah can't make up her mind what to think about my present state of mind. She alternates between being suitably shocked at my 'fanaticism' and wanting to share the fun herself. We now go to Communion together each Sunday, and despite an initial period of annoyance at all the formalities and rituals of the services, we both now enjoy them increasingly. To save one from becoming too drunk with the blood of Jesus, the prohibition laws of Madras State permit only sweetened grape juice! There has been a curious reversal of roles between Sarah and me. Previously she was the one who held 'irrational' beliefs about the supernatural and I used to tease her for her childish sentimentality. Now I am being childish — or perhaps adolescent — and it is her turn to be 'mature and sensible'.

I am fully aware that my present elation is only temporary. Like Peter, James, and John I shall soon be reluctantly forced down off the mountain to the dusty road below, to continue plodding the path of detachment. But that is all the more reason why I should make the most of being on the mountain now. Falling in love with a girl is just a foretaste of the deeper love which can develop through years of marriage, and the memory of that foretaste helps a married couple through the inevitable clashes and difficulties in their relationship. In the same way my elation at falling in love with Jesus is a small foretaste of the real joy to come when I eventually reach the Kingdom of Heaven, and having had that foretaste I am now all the more willing to endure the dusty road which leads there.

Postscript

POSTSCRIPT

We came home from India in May, on a coach only slightly less rickety than Brian's two years earlier. The water tank sprang a leak on the Khyber Pass, the dynamo konked out a few miles outside Tehran, and the coach skidded off a mud track which the driver had rashly taken as a short-cut through the mountains south of Trabzond. But with much shoving and swearing we managed to push it back onto the track rather than let it slide down into the river below. A legion of old coaches carrying penniless hippies now plies the route between London and Delhi, and the mountain roads through which they pass are littered with the rusting carcasses of local trucks and buses which have toppled over the edge. And yet to my knowledge no coach from London has ever suffered a similar fate. Jesus must look kindly on hippies.

The hippies on the return journey, however, are mostly disillusioned and homesick, Nirvana having somehow eluded them on the banks of the Ganges. We made particular friends with Dave from Bethnal Green. He had spent all his savings on the trip to India, but was so shocked by the apparent dishonesty, greed, and sheer lack of Nirvana among the Indians he met, that he was coming back after only three weeks. 'Every bloody Indian's trying to rip you off', he exclaimed. 'Hinduism hasn't done much for them. I'm gonna tell those Hare Krishna and Transcendental blokes in London to give up — they're flogging a dead horse.' In fact he and the other travellers were so keen to get back to the bliss of home that they pressed the driver to continue through the nights, and we stopped only five times between Tehran and Ostend.

June 25th passed without my even noticing it, for I now firmly thought of myself as a Christian. My mother recoiled in horror when I told her. She imagined that I would now become pro-Establishment, morally over-bearing and censorious, hypocritical, perhaps even a member of the Conservative Party — that I would throw out of the window all the ethical principles in which she so devoutly believes. Only quite recently has she come to accept that Christianity, in our case at least, can be combined with a sense of humour, socialist views, and a reasonable degree of moral sincerity. Towards Sarah's parents I had to swallow my pride, for having previously insisted that under no circumstances would I take Christian marriage vows, I was now keen to be married in church. And so we were, with Sarah dressed in blazing red hand-spun cotton from India.

We went back to our cottage in Durham, and while Sarah finished her degree, I spent my time trying to understand my new beliefs, with the help of the university theological library. The thing which concerned me most, and still does, is the relationship between Christians. Jesus is quite explicit that you cannot be a disciple alone — 'When two or three are gathered together...', 'I am the vine, and you are the branches' — and you must learn how to love and follow him together with other Christians. For practical purposes this means that you have to belong to a denomination, since that is how Christians are grouped. After much struggling, which included reading all the main speeches on in-fallibility from the Vatican Council of 1870, I decided that the special claims of the different denominations were spurious, and the only valid criterion in choosing between them is cultural affinity. However, I shelved the problem as to which denomination I should join

136

until last year when we settled in Lancaster. Then I finally admitted to myself that my own culture, even down to the Fabian brand of socialism that I espouse, sits most comfortably in the crumbling, dry-rot-ridden Anglican Church. And last March, to the surprise of our local congregation with whom I had been sharing Communion for the previous six months, I knelt beside the year's batch of choir boys and Sunday-school leavers to be confirmed by the Bishop of Blackburn.

But the question remains: what is the community of Christians, and how should it function? Jesus gives us almost no practical advice. The Acts of the Apostles, however, offers a thumb-nail sketch: 'They (the Christians in Jerusalem) met constantly to hear the apostles teach, and to share the common life, to break bread and to pray'; 'Not a man of them claimed any of his possessions as his own, but everything was held in common.' In other words there were three vital ingredients: common prayer, common study, and common finance.

Having once fallen in love with Jesus and felt the warmth of God, it is a matter of personal experience that prayer works better with other people. I now believe that praying for peace in Palestine, or praying for Mrs Brown with terminal cancer, actually helps Palestine or Mrs Brown. And that praying together with twenty-five other people is in some mysterious way more than twenty-five times as effective. Why God has instituted such a curious economy, encouraging us to form unions of beggars to plead more loudly, is beyond my understanding, except that it brings home to us our utter dependence on Him. But prayer is more than just begging. It is the art of loving an unseen bridegroom, who is infinitely polygamous, and we, the hopeful brides, must guide one another to the bridal chamber. The best guidance, of course, is from the successful lovers, the saints and mystics.

The Gospels were not printed across the sky by a great computer in the heavens, but were written by ordinary men. So, from the start, we learn about our Guru from other disciples. Logically, all other beliefs can follow from the single belief in the Holy Spirit, who guides the efforts of the Christian community to understand the truth. And once I could believe in the Holy Spirit, my previous worry about the historical accuracy of the Gospels evaporated: the Holy Spirit guided their writing and so for practical purposes the portrayal of Jesus is adequate. But it is little more than adequate, for we need the continuing help of the Holy Spirit to interpret our Guru's teaching. And since it would be vain to assume that the Holy Spirit will pay particular attention to me, this means that, like the Jerusalem Christians, I must hear the teachings of other experienced disciples.

Common finance is, of course, an embarrassment. We all believe, as Anglican communicants repeat each week, that 'all things come from you, and of your own do we give you', but since one cannot make out cheques to God, we easily ignore that He is the real owner of our assets. To the first Christians (or at least the ones described in the Acts) this meant devoting every penny to the Christian community, the body of Christ. But today the Church, unless you happen to be a monk, simply isn't geared for this kind of fanaticism: you are welcome to make handsome donations to the restoration fund or the children's home, but there is no opportunity to share all your possessions. Clearly in a complex modern economy with homes bought on mortgages, and wealth held in equities and life assurance policies, the simple financial arrangements of the Jerusalem community are not feasible. This doesn't matter because the purpose of sharing is not simply to equalise living standards among Christians, but rather to ensure that no Christian consumes more than he needs. 'The poor will be with you always', said Jesus, and while there are men in the world with no shirts on their backs, no Christian should have two shirts; all surplus income above the bare necessities must be given away. The reason, then, for devising some means of common ownership or pooling of income is that it's a great deal easier to make this sacrifice of love (and even learn to enjoy it!) as a group than on your own.

Until we settled down to the business of living in an ordinary parish I thought that Christians should all be friends, and that it was deception to speak of community without friendship. It is only since then that I have realised why close-knit monastic communities keep such strict rules of silence! Contrived Christian friendship — or 'fellowship' as it is euphemistically called — is both ridiculous to the outsider and insulting to the participants. Natural close friendships between individual Christians are vital, but the bond which embraces the whole Christian community does not depend on them. The bond is subtle and intangible, and Jesus himself could only express it in the sublime symbol of the Eucharist. The real difficulty lies in approaching the Eucharist in the right spirit, and making the symbol a reality; to gather round the Lord's table immersed not in private spiritual pleasures, but in peace and with an open heart towards one's fellow disciples. And this requires not smiles and pleasantries, but a conscious recognition that Jesus loves the old woman in the next pew who champs her false teeth, and the stiff-necked man who thinks vandals should be flogged, just as dearly as he loves me.

*   *   *

I am now, as you may gather, on the dusty road beneath Mount Tabor. I love but am no longer in love. I have grown more accustomed to the presence of Jesus, and more practised at making decisions and adjusting my life accordingly. But I am still a novice, and in dark, apathetic moments find myself doubting my faith. When this happens I go back to my first utilitarian principles. I want to be happy. Therefore I had best follow the example of someone who is himself happy. And I need only read a few chapters of the Gospels to remind myself how profoundly happy Jesus was.